DISTINCTION EARNED

CAPE BRETON'S BOXING LEGENDS 1946-1970

BY PAUL MACDOUGALL

Cape Breton University Press
Sydney, Nova Scotia

DISTINCTION EARNED

CAPE BRETON'S BOXING LEGENDS 1946-1970

BY PAUL MACDOUGALL

Cape Breton University Press
Sydney, Nova Scotia

Cape Breton University Press recognizes the support of Canada Council for the Arts and of the Province of Nova Scotia, through the Department of Tourism, Culture and Heritage. We are pleased to work in partnership with these bodies to develop and promote our cultural resources.

Canada Council   Conseil des Arts
for the Arts   du Canada

NOVA SCOTIA

Tourism, Culture and Heritage

Cover design: Cathy MacLean, Pleasant Bay, NS
Cover images: See the following pages for credits:
        Front, clockwise from upper right – p. 119, p. 76, p. 38, p. 28, p. 140, p. 142.
        Back, top to bottom – p. 134, p. 139, p. 139, p. 23.
Layout: Mike Hunter, Port Hawkesbury and Sydney, NS
Printed in Canada by Marquis Imprimeur

Library and Archives Canada Cataloguing in Publication

MacDougall, Paul, 1959-
Distinction earned : Cape Breton's boxing legends, 1946-1970 / Paul
MacDougall.

Includes bibliographical references and index.
ISBN 978-1-897009-48-2

1. Boxers (Sports)--Nova Scotia--Cape Breton Island--Biography.
2. Boxing--Nova Scotia--Cape Breton Island--History. I. Title.

GV1131.M33 2010   796.83092'27169   C2010-905010-X

Cape Breton University Press
P.O. Box 5300
Sydney, NS B1P 6L2

DISTINCTION EARNED
CAPE BRETON BOXING LEGENDS 1946 TO 1970

This book was written for the Cape Breton Boxing Fraternity,
and in memory of Earle Pemberton, sportswriter, and Graham MacKay, sports fan.

PRE FIGHT WARM UP

This is a true story about a time and place that no longer exists. It's peopled with real characters who bore witness to triumph and tragedy. It's a story for and about the people of Cape Breton Island who lived through the devastation of two World Wars and found solace in a mutual brotherhood. It's a tale of strength, heart, courage and resilience, of clean living and hard living, of set backs, injuries and untimely deaths. It's a collective memoir about some of the toughest, yet most humble men you could ever meet. And it's a story of victory and its often present companion, loss.

This story begins in 1920, in Whitney Pier, a rough and tough, hardscrabble area of Sydney, Cape Breton, Nova Scotia. In "the Pier," nearly everyone worked at the local steel plant, which was one of the most state-of-the-art facilities in the world at the time. The people of the Pier lived off the food from their neighbourhood gardens, relied on their friends and families when the going got tough, and basically led good, albeit sometimes hard, lives. They were from the West Indies, numerous European countries, and the yet-to-be confederated colony of Newfoundland. Many of the immigrants from Italy, Poland, he Ukraine and other parts of Europe had come to Nova Scotia to escape the carnage and madness of the First World War. Solid, hardworking folk, by the thousands they came and stayed. They were as strong and resilient as the nails, wire and rails produced by the steel plant that so many of them relied on for a living. It was here, in Whitney Pier, in this long lost time that one of Cape Breton's greatest triumphs began. It was in this time, and in this place, that our story begins with a man named Joe Uvanni.

Uvanni was of Italian descent and had grown up in the Bronx area of New York. He came to Sydney around 1920 and began to go around with other Italians emigrants living in the Pier. One place Uvanni could often be found was in a store owned by the Delvecchio family. The Delvecchios also ran a bakery, which was adjacent to their store. Their businesses were located on Tupper Street, just off Victoria Road, the main thoroughfare in the Pier, not far from the coke ovens of the steel plant. As those who've ever visited old buildings like Delvecchio's will know, you may often discover there's an out-of-the-way upstairs office, or a series of backrooms, or a long, dingy hallway that may connect two adjacent buildings. As these buildings were often places of business, sometimes there's even a warehouse attached. These features are not uncommon in buildings constructed at the turn of the 20th century along Victoria Road in the Pier. It was in these smoky, dimly lit rooms where real stories unfolded, backroom stories that had little or nothing to do with the actual business of the store. Indeed, if one were to go back in time and peer through a dusty window of Delvecchio's warehouse, circa 1921, one might be likely to see two nearly naked men, sweaty and glistening, locked in an embrace. Sounds like a good place to start a story, eh? Perhaps the greatest Cape Breton sports story never told.

One of those two men locked in that embrace in that backroom at Delvecchio's was a young man by the name of Johnny Nemis. The other fellow, we don't know; he may have been any one of a dozen or so young men who went around with Joe Uvanni. It doesn't really matter who he was. What matters is that these men were boxing. What matters is that when they broke their clinch and started to throw hard jabs, devastating hooks and jaw-rattling uppercuts, Johnny Nemis was the one left standing. Nemis, barely out of his teens in that backroom, would go on to become one of the most influential figures in Cape Breton boxing history. First as fighter: then, more profoundly, as a trainer. And while the boxers, trainers and promoters you are about to meet follow a sequence of training, amateur fights, pro bouts and ultimately Canadian and British Empire boxing championships, it can all be traced back to the early days of Johnny Nemis, the boy from New Waterford, Cape Breton, who got his start dancing, punching and clinching in that musty warehouse gym with Joe Uvanni from New York.

In 2003, 93-year-old Mike Tortola[1] of Sydney spoke of Joe Uvanni's arrival. "Joe Uvanni came down to the Pier to train Nicholas 'Hawkey' Delvecchio," who was a well-known up and coming boxer at the time.[2] Delvecchio started boxing in 1921 at the age of twelve on the advice of his father Tony who said, "[i]f you want to fight, don't do it for nothing, box in the ring." As a youngster Delvecchio worked at Jake Levitan's grocery store and trained upstairs at Martinello's Hall on Tupper Street. According to Tortola: "Down there (the Pier) at that time there was prosperity for boxing. There were ten, eleven or twelve boxers that [Uvanni] used to train with.

Uvanni was an expert. He was a trainer in the States. He didn't fight here. He just trained whoever wanted to be in his club. There was a police club also but not many people went there." Hawkey Delvecchio liked Uvanni because, as Tortola puts it, "[h]e knew a lot of the tricks of the trade." Tortola explained that Uvanni used to go back and forth to the States on a frequent basis but liked Sydney because there was a great interest in boxing here at that time. "I bet there was a fight every fifteen days in Sydney back then," said Tortola.

At the time of Uvanni's arrival in Sydney boxing was quite established and Cape Breton already had its fair share of local boxing heros. These included the likes of Jack Munroe, Mickey MacIntyre, Bernard "Kid" O'Neill, Johnny Gillis, Jack McKenna and Stevie "Kid" MacDonald and his six battling brothers. Mainland Nova Scotia also had many successful boxers at the time including Sam Langford from Weymouth Falls, considered boxing's greatest uncrowned champion by sportswriter Clay Moyle, and George Dixon from Halifax.[3]

Jack Munroe was a legendary Cape Bretoner in and out of the boxing ring.[4] He was a prospector in Ontario, served in the First World War and was honored by the King of England and the Canadian Parliament for his heroic deeds, which he wrote about in a book entitled *Mopping Up*. In his short career as a boxer he is most remembered for going four rounds in an exhibition match with James J. Jeffries, the reigning world heavyweight champion. He knocked Jeffries down in the fourth, allowing him to claim a $1000 prize for completing the fight. In a second bout between the two, Jeffries won in the second round. Mickey MacIntyre, "The Pride of Cape Breton" was born in 1890 and began boxing in 1907.[5] He was befriended in Boston by Sam Langford who helped him with his first few fights. He fought many great boxers of the day throughout Canada and the United States and eventually became Welterweight Champion of Canada. Described as a likeable chap with a heart the size of a football McIntyre spent most of his winnings on his legion of friends and unfortunately died at the age of thirty-two after a battle with pneumonia.

Bernard "Kid" O'Neill, was born in 1890 in Halifax and moved to Sydney as a child with his parents.[6] He fought from 1907 to 1917 eventually becoming Lightweight

Fig. 0.1. Jack Munroe and James Jeffries. Courtesy Jake MacKinnon.

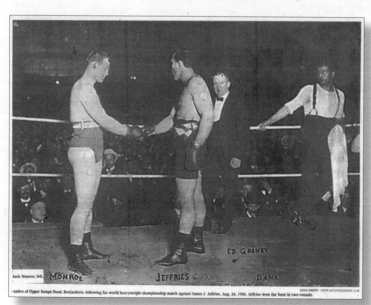

Champion of the Maritimes. He fought Billy Parsons to five draws over his career. Ironically Mickey MacIntyre claimed Parsons hit him harder than anyone, while O'Neill never was hurt by Parsons over the course of their five ring battles. In a colourful post-boxing career O'Neill became a dancehall maestro, ran the legendary Derby tavern on Gottingen Street in Halifax for years and was active in rum running during prohibition, making regular sailing trips on his boat to St. Pierre et Miquelon and Cuba to pick up liquor and return it to Nova Scotia. He even had dealings with mobster Al Capone during this time, who he described as, "not a bad guy in some ways."

Johnny Gillis hailed from Dominion and began fighting in 1914 as a lightweight, eventually winning the Maritime Championship.[7] He fought against numerous opponents before leaving boxing to study engineering. He went on to become a chief engineer for the Dominion Coal Company. Stevie "Kid" MacDonald was from Glace Bay and began fighting a couple of years after Gillis.[8] He racked up a considerable ring record over 29 years of boxing and 187 bouts. For a period of time both he and fellow Cape Breton boxer Jack McKenna lived together in Cleveland and trained with Eddie Mead. Northside native McKenna himself went on to become one of the toughest boxers to ever come out of Cape Breton. George Dixon was the first Black man to win a world title under the Marquis of Queensberry Rules when he beat Nunc Wallace for the World Bantamweight Crown in 1890 in London, England.[9] Dixon was famous for his endurance in the ring and fought and won a 70 round fight earlier that same year against Cal McCarthy in Boston. He once fought and won three fights with three different opponents over a five day period.

Fig. 0.2.
Mickey MacIntyre.
Courtesy Jake
MacKinnon.

Other notable boxers who be-gan their career in the Cape Breton rings of the 1920s included Maurice "Blue" MacDonald, Joe "Tip Top" Smith, Alex MacNeil, Dannie Boutilier, Alex MacKay and Bobbie Jackson.[10] Maurice MacDonald was known for his three memorable fights against Canadian Middleweight champ Jack McKenna. He drew in the first match, lost the second by decision after ten rounds and was stopped by McKenna in the eighth round with three broken ribs. Aside from being a well known Glace Bay haberdasher in his later years Joe Smith could claim that he had the world record for one round knockdowns after he put Walter Roachville to the mat nine times in an amateur match at the Boston Gardens in 1930.[11]

With this rich tradition of boxing in Cape Breton to draw upon it is easy to understand why a boxer turned trainer such as Joe Uvanni would chose Sydney as a likely place to ply his trade. The movement of boxers from Cape Breton to New England and especially the Boston area was quite established, therefore Uvanni would have been well aware of the success of Cape Breton boxers both at home and abroad. Getting involved in the Cape Breton fight game would not have been considered a bad bet in the early days of the 1920s. From local newspaper articles as early as 1922, it appears Uvanni was already established as a fight promoter in Sydney. He was a veteran of the ring himself, having fought more than 150 amateur and professional bouts. He fought the famous Nova Scotian boxer of the day, Roddy "Big Pay" MacDonald on two occasions, losing one and battling to a draw in the other. Uvanni told George MacEachern, a young boxer at the time (who went on to become a legendary Cape Breton labor leader), that he

Fig. 0.3. Joe Uvanni. Photographer unknown. Photo: Antiquities of the Prize Ring. www.antekprizering.com/

woke up the morning after a fight with MacDonald and didn't even know where he was.[12] MacEachern recalls "He said, 'Boy what a punch that fellow's got, I better get over and sign him up.' Joe was getting old himself and he figured he'd get someone else to do the fighting."

When Uvanni eventually settled in Sydney he first worked out of Delvecchio's, and then began training in a gym further down the Pier on Dominion Street. Eventually, according to Mike Tortola, "[t]he police were after him to train," and so he started working as an instructor with the Sydney Police Club on Charlotte Street in downtown Sydney. At the time there was no local boxing commission, therefore it was up to Uvanni to schedule fights and select the opponents while the police club hosted the bouts.

From a description in *The Sydney Post* of a rather one-sided bout between Jack McKenna of North Sydney and Peter Hines of Glace Bay, it appears Uvanni was as interested in making money as he was in training boxers.[13] McKenna, a well-known and incredibly powerful puncher, destroyed the overmatched Hines. The article stated: "It was the case of a hard hitting scientific boxer up against a tough unpolished slugger." Not all of the boxing was as explosive as that brought on by the likes of the hard-hitting McKenna. Earlier on the same card, George MacEachern, just a kid at the time, took on an opponent named Charlie Smith in a match in which there was, according to the paper, "not a blow struck in the whole four rounds that would have hurt a kitten."

In his 1987 autobiography, *The Story of a Cape Breton Radical*, George MacEachern, who states he had a "consuming interest" in boxing, describes those early days of training with Joe Uvanni.

"Joe Uvanni used to teach us that the right hand went for defensive purposes unless you had a sure thing. Use your left hand. But your right hand was always across your chest, your elbow in close and your hand across like that and your toes turned in. I remember that routine alright. Your toes were turned in for balance. Joe was a wonderful trainer except the son of a bitch would take money from people. He never took any from me. I got my lessons free because I used to work out with his victims to make him look good. He couldn't lose if he did get a few punches in the nose as long as the kid's father felt it was improvement. But Joe would give them one lesson you see. It was $12 a lesson, and then he couldn't be found after that."[14]

**GEORGE MacEACHERN:
An Autobiography**

The Story Of
A Cape Breton Radical

Fig. 0.4. George MacEachern's autobiography: *The Story of a Cape Breton Radical.*

In a transcript of a 1978 interview with Cape Breton University historian Donald MacGillivray, MacEachern recalls being in the dressing room after the one-sided McKenna-Hines bout.[15] MacEachern states that Hines folded up in a heap on the canvas as referee Billy Parsons, a former boxer himself, immediately awarded the fight to McKenna and declared all bets on the bout were off. Parsons came into the dressing room and demanded his pay from Joe Uvanni for refereeing the non-event.

Uvanni told Parsons there was no money coming to him and implied the fight wasn't on the up and up. Parsons confronted Uvanni and, according to MacEachern, "Joe hit him with the heel of his hand in the side of the head. Well I expected to see the head going.... I doubt if he ever got the $25 for the refereeing."

In 1921, Johnny Nemis, seriously infected with the boxing bug, heard Joe Uvanni was training boxers in the Pier and so paid him a visit. Uvanni saw potential in the young upstart and, likely recognizing a way to make some money and train a good fighter, quickly took him in. Nemis came from a town named Nimis, near the provincial capital of Udine in northeastern Italy.[16] Born in 1904, he came to Canada in 1905 as a babe in arms and settled in Glace Bay with his parents, Giuseppe (Joe) and Enrica Nemis. According to Sally Durando, Johnny Nemis's niece, Joe and Enrica had a daughter, Rena, they had left behind in Italy, but who eventually joined them in Canada some years later. Joe Nemis was a miner and often served as an interpreter for his fellow Italian miners. In 1907 the Nemis family welcomed a second son, Dominic, followed quickly by a third, Louie, in 1908.

In 1910, the Nemis family moved to the neighbouring coal boom town of New Waterford. By 1920 the Nemis family had grown to seven children, Johnny, Dominic, Louie, James (Cookie), Anna, Rena and Eta. Johnny by then was living in Halifax at a place called St. Patrick's Home.[17] The home was connected with the Christian Brothers, a Catholic Church group known for working with people dealing with problems and issues that presented challenges to themselves and their families. The reason why Nemis was sent to live with the Christian Brothers in 1920 is unknown, but whatever got him there also put him on a life's path of boxing. Boxing was a source of discipline and physical fitness for this sect of the church and, later on, many priests used boxing as a way to keep kids out of trouble. Mike Tortola remembers a priest from Iona, Father MacLean, who also liked boxing and came to be priest at St. Nicholas Church in the Pier. He enjoyed training at the Delvecchio ring in Whitney Pier. "He was a rough and tough man," said Tortola of the padre. This early influence of religion may also have touched the young fighter from new Waterford because his niece Sally Durando remembers him as a devout catholic who was always saying the rosary.[18]

Whenever good boxers appeared on cards in Halifax, the Christian Brothers always arranged for them to visit St. Patrick's Home. Noted fighters of the day such as Mike McTigue, Jeff Smith, Roddie MacDonald and Leo Hauck all visited the home and spent time teaching the boys some of their skills. Watching these boxers fight in Halifax left an impression on the 16-year-old Nemis that would never fade. "We staged quite a number of battle royals," recalled Johnny. "The Christian Brother instructor would blow the whistle and shout, 'Ok boys, go to it, nutbars and peanuts to the winner'."

At the time Johnny Nemis was getting interested in boxing in Halifax, Whitney Pier was a "hotbed of fistiana," as Kid O'Neill remembers it. "My first experience was gained as a schoolboy with the schoolyard or nearby vacant lot as our first ring," O'Neill related to Earle Pemberton, sportswriter, publisher and boxing guru from Glace Bay, in 1964.[19]

Earle Pemberton was born in Windsor, Nova Scotia, and came to Glace Bay at a young age with his family.[20] He was an electrician by trade who worked on his own, and had literally no school education at all. He often boasted to his son Edward, "I've been working since I was eight years old." Edward said. "Education never interfered with him." Pemberton's interest in boxing went back to his younger days and, when he was committed to a wheel chair later in life because of bad arthritis, he turned to writing and selling his publication as a way to make a modest income. Pemberton was a well-read man and *Punching with Pemberton*, in addition to recording the boxing news of the day, was also peppered with poetry written by him and other writers, as well as features on other sporting events and activities with a Cape Breton connection. The local newspapers at that time covered boxing, but *Punching with Pemberton* put boxing in a historical perspective and copies that remain today are a great source of research material for boxing enthusiasts. Nat Fleischer the founding editor of *Ring Magazine*, long considered the bible of boxing and still in publication today, read *Punching with Pemberton* himself and considered it an "excellent" sports publication.[21]

Pemberton's piece on O'Neill continued with O'Neill recalling, "They weren't grudge fights; on the contrary, we youngsters who lived in the constant atmosphere of fight talk, and we arranged matches as we arranged pick-up games of hockey or baseball." O'Neill fought fifty advertised fights before he hung up his gloves in 1917, and they weren't "panty waste affairs," according to him. "Most were for fifteen rounds, some were for twenty," and the "fans wanted action. If you provided it, they were with you. If you failed to do so, they wouldn't go see you again." Promoters at the time couldn't always get a prize fight "sanctioned" so they'd fight in private halls and occasionally, as O'Neill related to Pemberton, "in a stable where the horses had been chased out, the stalls dismantled and a temporary ring erected." O'Neill recalls having been very fond of the fight game because he and others fought more than once in such fights for nothing, just to prove they could lick the other guy.

Fig. 0.5. Dick Wagner, Jack Dempsey and Earle Pemberton at Sydney Forum. 1960. Photographer unknown. Courtesy Tyrone Gardiner.

By the 1920s there was lots of boxing action to be had in Cape Breton for anyone inclined to the sport. In a *Cape Breton Post* article from the 1970s, John Campbell describes every town as having their favorite fighters as well as promoters. "The not so friendly rivalries helped to maintain consistently high attendance at frequent cards," wrote Campbell. George MacEachern recalls the Cape Breton boxing scene in the early 1920s.

It was quite a sport and good boxers could fill the halls. There was Bobby "Kid" Smith and Jack McKenna; they fought over in the rink at North Sydney. They filled the place. We had a lot of good boys on the go in those days. Some of them, Stevie Kid and his two brothers, they fought in the big time in the States.

"Any day in the week would find me at the boxing club working out with fighters or, on a few occasions, preparing for a fight of my own. I never got to be a champion or anything of the sort. I liked to work out with the fellows in the gym. I didn't find many people my size. I only weighed 118 pounds anyway. If there were muscles they weren't visible. But I could get around fairly fast and I liked it. It was lop-sided, it was generally with bigger people. This was real enjoyment to me. I still enjoy it… I think it did me a world of good. It did a lot of good for my health and a lot for my confidence."

Though George MacEachern only fought eight fights in his brief boxing career, his reasons for getting into the sport epitomized the reasons the other young men of the 1920s and subsequent years also climbed into the ring. In MacEachern's words, "It was good. I'll tell you a fellow never realizes what it is to live until he's fit; in good physical condition from exercise." It was into this exciting and dynamic milieu of boxing, training, promoters, trainers, tough guys and fight talk that young men like Johnny Nemis and his brothers were quickly drawn. According to Mike Tortola, Johnny Nemis was "a very good boxer who trained under Joe Uvanni … and seemed to know just as much if not more than Uvanni."

Tortola also explained how Joe Uvanni came to leave Sydney. "He thought these boxers would fight every night. Joe wanted to make his living on this and he got disappointed when they didn't. When he went away he didn't tell anyone he wasn't going to come back. He said I'm going back to the States because I want to see someone and I'll be back. And that was it. He never came back." Tortola felt that although Uvanni left, "Nemis didn't disgrace him. "In fact, that's the time when Johnny Nemis became really experienced in boxing."

Tortola recalls that Uvanni had no wife or family with him while he was training in Sydney, and whether he had any family in New York he didn't know. Though he came and went in a rather short period of time, Joe Uvanni and the old warehouse gym in Whitney Pier gave Johnny Nemis his start in boxing and, while Uvanni may never have realized it, he had helped to get underway one of the greatest Canadian sports stories of the 20th century.

ROUND ONE:
JOHNNY NEMIS

Like many young men of his day and age in Industrial Cape Breton, Johnny Nemis made his living working in the coalmines that surrounded the rugged yet beautiful coastline of New Waterford. Stretching for miles under the Atlantic Ocean, the coal seams of Cape Breton supplied food, clothing and shelter for thousands of people for more than a hundred years. Johnny himself began working in Number 15 colliery at the now unheard of age of thirteen. He worked at Number 14 and Number 16 mines, as well, until war broke out in 1940.

In 1922, at the age of eighteen, Johnny Nemis was ready for his first fight. He fought Norman Elcock at the Italian Hall at No. 14, a district in New Waterford. Nemis put Elcock to the mat in the fourth round. A year later, Johnny's last sibling was born, a brother, Joe who went by the nickname Bougie.

In Sam Migliore and A. Evo DiPierro's book, *Italian Lives, Cape Breton Memories*, Joe Nemis, who eventually became "the last of the fighting Nemises," recounted how his two older brothers, Johnny and Louie, used to workout in the field adjacent to their home in New Waterford.[1] "They'd start boxing, and it would turn to war. Louie

Fig. 1.1. The Nemis family of New Waterford. Back row (left to right): Anna, James (Cookie), Dominic and Louie. Front row: Rena, Joseph (Sr.), Enrica (mother) with Joseph on her lap, Eta and Johnny. Ca. 1926. Family photo courtesy Sally Durando (Anna's daughter).

could punch like Rocky Graziano. He used to break bones. But Johnny was more of a boxer." Mrs. Nemis never liked to see the boys fighting and on at least one occasion put an end to their match by resorting to a mother's best defensive stance—tears. The aversion to boxing wasn't just limited to Mrs. Nemis. In later years her daughter Anna had threatened to cut her Uncle Johnny off meals and visits to the house if he ever got her son Guido interested in boxing. According to Anna's daughter Sally Durando, the threat of no more Italian bean soup was enough to keep Johnny at bay in his later years as a trainer.[2]

But in 1926, Johnny Nemis had more than bean soup on his mind and was well on his way to becoming one of New Waterford's local heroes. Nemis is described as the pride of New Waterford after he won a ten round decision against Nedder Healey of Halifax in a fight held in New Glasgow early in the year. It was one of the biggest tournaments of 1926 and a large crowd had packed the theatre where it was held. Of Johnny Nemis, the *Sydney Post* quoted a New Glasgow writer who stated:

"Probably no boxer who has visited New Glasgow is in better shape physically than the nineteen year old Italian boy. He is as hard as nails… a picture of good health and perfect training. He is careful with his diet, trains daily, does not smoke or hit the hops, and looks like a boy who will go far in the fight game."[3]

Fig. 1.2. Johnny Nemis. Courtesy Karl Marsh.

That same year Jack McKenna of North Sydney was the Maritime Welterweight Champion. Nemis's success throughout the year made him a worthy opponent for McKenna. A fight was scheduled between the two homegrown boys at the old Savoy Theatre in Glace Bay.[4] In order to get New Waterford fight fans to the card, a special train of five coaches was hooked up to a Sydney and Louisburg Railway locomotive. In addition, the tram company ran three specials in order to bring in fight hungry fans from Sydney, while people from elsewhere on the island made their way, one way or another, to Glace Bay that night.

McKenna weighed in at 146 pounds and Nemis at 145, both in top condition. According to Earle Pemberton, the fight between champion and challenger was fairly even throughout. Referee Tommy Casey had to warn McKenna twice for fouling and McKenna began to miss with his punches as the fight wore on. Nemis though, was described by Pemberton as "coolness personified," and "his timing was perfect and he handled himself like a veteran when in trouble." McKenna got wilder as the fight wore on and that, with the combination of fouls incurred, gave the decision to Nemis, to great applause from the 1,500 fans in attendance that night.

Nemis's prowess in the ring was not unnoticed by some of the great boxers of the day. Nova Scotia born Sam Langford, described as one of the hardest punches of all time by Nat Fleischer of *Ring Magazine* and as the greatest pound for pound boxer that ever lived by boxing writer Hype Igoe, had on at least one occasion spent time with Nemis and his New Waterford training entourage.[5] On one occasion, although the date is uncertain, it appears that Langford visited Nemis in his hometown during Nemis's preparation for an upcoming fight.

Allie Steele of Sydney, former president of Boxing Nova Scotia and veteran of sixty-three fights himself, began his training with Johnny Nemis in the 1940s.[6] "Johnny was very strong with knowing how to defend yourself," Steele recalls. As a trainer, "Johnny Nemis was head and shoulders over the rest because he could really teach you the basics and you learned them well. You'd start off with the footwork, then learn to jab properly. It's like trying to learn algebra without some basic knowledge of math—you can't do it."

It was these skills that Nemis first picked up with Joe Uvanni and later honed on his own that pushed him into the spotlight of the Cape Breton fight game of the 1920s. Nemis was so respected that in 1927, prior to leaving for the United States for a number of scheduled matches, the tightly knit business community of New Waterford held a private reception for their favourite son and gave him as gifts an engraved watch and a suitcase. While this may pale to the garish swag modern day fighters might acquire, that watch and that suitcase were a true heartfelt gesture that let Nemis know his entire hometown was behind him, rooting for him and wishing him well.

A couple of weeks after arriving in Boston, Nemis fought Spike Hennessey, a highly rated New England welterweight. Within six rounds it was over for Hennessey. Most of the boxers

Fig. 1.3. Back row (left to right): unidentified, Angelo DeGiobbi, Alan Deino DeGiobbi, Sam Langford, unidentified. Front row: unidentified, Johnny Nemis, James (Cookie) Nemis. Ca. 1920s. Courtesy Sally Durando.

Fig. 1.4. Allie Steele, courtesy Leo MacDonald.

around Worcester, Massachusetts at the time were handled by Harvey Dodge. Dodge assigned a couple of regular sparring partners to Johnny. One of these sparring partners was Lou Bogash.

In *Punching with Pemberton*, Earle Pemberton wrote that Nemis liked to talk about how his first sparring session with Bogash went. In Johnny's words: "There was a big heavy brass cuspidor on the floor of the gym in which the boxers used to spit. Just before my first sparring session with Mr. Bogash I watched him pound hell out of a young fellow and when he was finished he pointed to me and said, 'OK sonny boy, you're next—and if you try any of your rough stuff on me I'll crown you with the contents of the cuspidor'."

After fighting a number of successful bouts in New England, Nemis returned to Cape Breton for an October, 1928, rematch against Jack McKenna. Over the past two years while Johnny was slugging it out in New England, McKenna was packing it on in Cape Breton. McKenna jumped a weight class to middleweight by weighing in at 165 pounds, almost 20 pounds more than when he had first fought Nemis two years earlier. Nemis weighed in at 146 pounds, only a pound heavier than his 1926 weight. At the time of Nemis's return to Cape Breton, McKenna was already on line to fight one of the world's leading middleweights, the American Ace Hudkins, known to fight fans as The Nebraska Wildcat.

Nemis recounted the fateful rematch with McKenna in the August 1964 issue of *Punching with Pemberton*. The fight was staged in the old curling rink in Sydney and Melvin McPhee was Johnny's handler at the time. As Nemis described it to Pemberton, "In the third round I started to work on the inside. McKenna caught me a wicked one back of the ear. I almost blacked out. When the cobwebs started to clear and my senses began to come back I thought to myself, this fellow sure clipped me good."

Nemis went on to describe the remaining fight. "I don't remember the fourth round at all and here I am in the fifth. I'll have to watch him and see that he doesn't connect that way again. I'll be all right in a couple of rounds. The bell rang, ending what I thought was the fifth; in reality it was the end of the tenth. The fight was over. In this fight I hit the deck six times for the count of nine." The Nemis-McKenna ten-round rematch decision went to McKenna. McKenna was the first fighter to send Johnny Nemis to the canvas. McKenna was fighting at his best during this time period and Nemis was the only fighter who was able to go the distance with him.[7]

In a press report written up the next day after the fight, the writer stated that "the New Waterford boy is one of the gamest fighters ever seen here. All doubts as to whether he could 'take it' were cleared up. Take it he did through the ten long rounds that must have been centuries to him. It is reported that from the third to the tenth round he did not know he was in the ring. His mind was a complete blank." The article went on to say that, "his stout heart and gameness carried him through and saved him from the ignominy of a knockout, never before suffered by Nemis."

By 1930, Johnny Nemis was boxing in approximately three bouts every two months. That year he took the Maritime Middleweight title from Joe Irvin of Saint John, New Brunswick. This was his seventh straight win over the rugged New Brunswicker. In the next few years Nemis fought a number of classic matches and rematches with many of the great fighters of the day. One set of fights was a trio of bouts against fellow New Waterforder, Buddie Lewis.

According to Pemberton, there was little love lost between the two local heroes. The first ten-round match ended in a draw, while Lewis took the next two fights. At the termination of a close match, Nemis stormed out of the ring yelling, "Lock both of us in a freight car and whoever comes out first will be declared the winner." Nemis's desire to fight in a boxcar was fitting. Allie Steele recounts Nemis telling him that when he was taking the train to Halifax or Maine to fight, he would ask the conductor to let him use an empty boxcar to train in on the way up. "He used to do shadow boxing and keep loose on the way instead of just sitting around. He had quite a boxing head on him, you know," said Steele.

Johnny Nemis also fought a trio of bouts against Maurice MacDonald, with the rubber match proving to be one of the toughest fights of his career. "I must have been floored about a dozen times," Nemis told Pemberton, though he still came out the winner on a foul in the seventh round. The first two fights were held in the curling rink in Sydney, with a draw in the first bout and a decision for Nemis in the second. The third and toughest fight was held in Glace Bay at the Russell Theatre. Broken nose aside, Nemis was the victor.

By the early 1930s, Nemis had amassed well over 200 fights, winning the vast majority of them. According to his brother, Joe "The Hammer" Nemis, also a boxer of repute, Johnny may have lost as few as thirteen fights, and over the course of those 200 bouts was never knocked out. Joe believed Johnny attempted to retire from the ring in 1934, but came back in 1936. He remembers his brother knocking out David Smith in Sydney Mines and winning another fight at the Fireman's Hall in Glace Bay in 1937.

On New Year's Day, 1938, Johnny Nemis fought his last fight back in New Waterford, where he had made his professional debut so many years before. He battled to a ten-round draw against Earl Kinsman at St. Agnes Gym. Due to failing eyesight, this was the last time Johnny Nemis would enter the ring as a fighter. In all, he fought his way through 278 battles over sixteen years, an average of three fights per month—hardly conceivable for a boxer today.

Regarded by many in the boxing community as someone who really understood the sport, it soon became evident to Johnny, having retired from the ring for good in 1938, that he should turn his attention to training. One of the earliest boxers to train with Johnny Nemis was Sailor Don MacKinnon. Mackinnon was born in 1923 in the tiny community of Deepvale, near the village of Inverness, Cape Breton.

MacKinnon had an interest in boxing from an early age and often hit a homemade punching bag that he had filled with sand from Inverness beach. He hung the heavy bag from a tree branch in a clearing in the woods behind his home. He'd wrap towels around his young hands to try to avoid damaging his knuckles, but most times when he went back inside his fists would be stained red with blood.

At the age of sixteen, after spending a year working in the Inverness coal mines, MacKinnon sent Johnny Nemis a picture of himself and asked him if he'd be interested in training him. Nemis was well known throughout Cape Breton and his name was forever in the sports pages of local newspapers. In his 1996 autobiography, *The Fighting Sailor*, MacKinnon noted: "He wrote back and said, 'Well come on down and I'll train you.' I then quit the mines.[8] My Father never said anything about me leaving. The day when I left my Mother felt bad. She didn't like it but felt, 'let him do what he wants. He gets hurt, he might quit'."

MacKinnon had saved ninety dollars while working in the mines and took that money with him when he moved to New Waterford. He boarded with a relative and spent a month training with Nemis. In his autobiography, MacKinnon recalled his first formal training sessions with Nemis.

Fig. 1.5. *The Fighting Sailor*.

THE FIGHTING SAILOR:

The Autobiography of Sailor Don McKinnon Pride of Saint John New Brunswick

Don McKinnon with Peter McGahan

"Johnny trained me during that month. He trained many fighters after he quit boxing in 1938. He had me shadow boxing. He had me skipping rope. He had me hit the heavy bag out in the yard. I sparred with other fighters including Joey Nemis, his brother. Early every morning I ran a quarter of a mile or half a mile. Johnny said, 'I'll put your name in the paper in a couple of weeks' time.' It came natural to me. Johnny told me that I could go a long ways. A year later when I was fighting down in Maine and he read about it in the papers, he told them at home that it was too bad I didn't stay with him because he would have made a good fighter out of me. He said I was tough and I could take it when I got knocked out."

Sailor Don MacKinnon gained his moniker in 1939 when he joined the navy, one year underage, after seeing sailors on the streets of Sydney and admiring their uniforms. He boxed as an amateur in the navy and turned pro after the war. He fought in Montreal and in New Brunswick, and so often in Maine that he became known as the "busiest fighter in the state of Maine." In *Beyond Heroes: A Sport History of Nova Scotia*, author Sandy Young says McKinnon was suspended from boxing in Providence, Rhode Island, for fighting three times in one week under three different names.[9] Like Nemis, McKinnon eventually became a trainer and settled in Saint John, New Brunswick.

With the advent of war in Europe, Johnny Nemis, like his young trainee MacKinnon, enlisted for service. And then, in 1940, Nemis was given the task of boxing instructor for the Canadian army. There had been a long tradition of boxing in the military when Nemis enlisted, a tradition that was unilaterally cancelled in 1964 due to political interference. But in 1940, boxing was hugely popular in the military and plenty of recruits were interested. Nemis taught five and six classes in boxing per day. At one time he had as many as 90 students. Joe Nemis remembers Johnny getting leave from the army so he could come home to train Joe, who as the youngest boxing Nemis was just getting ready to embark on his fighting career. "He (Johnny) used to train me so hard that I couldn't lift my hands. I was too weak to fight. The fellow rubbing me down would tell me that he could see ice water coming out of me. Cold sweat!"

Joe Nemis recounted in *Italian Lives* that in his first amateur fight in 1942 he was training under his brother, Johnny. "I turned my head to wink at someone and all of a sudden, *wham*.... I heard the referee counting four, five, I got up and I stayed right in close until the round ended." This was only the first round. Joe "The Hammer" stuck out the fight and lost in a decision, but was awarded the trophy for most outstanding boxer of the tournament because he was able to battle back after a first-round knock-down. Forty other boxers competed for this same trophy. Joe credits his fighting skills to his ability to stay in close, thereby depriving your opponent of any form of leverage, which he learned from watching older brother Johnny over the years.

That same year, Johnny Nemis was also responsible for training the New Waterford Mount Carmel boxing team, which went on to compete in the Maritime Amateur Championships in Halifax. Two featherweights, Leo Fahey and Oliver Geldart, beat everyone in their class and were left to face each other in the title match. Earle Pemberton stated that the distasteful decision to allow fellow club mates to fight each other was left up to Nemis to make. He allowed the match and the fight ended with a decision going to Fahey.

By the late 1940s and into the 1950s, boxing had become a huge sporting activity in Cape Breton. Fight crazy fans would spend days talking about upcoming bouts and would pack halls, boxing clubs and hockey

Fig. 1.6. Joe Nemis. Courtesy Karl Marsh.

rinks to capacity to see their local boys slug it out. Many matches featured fighters from the rest of the province as well as the entire Atlantic region, with numerous title bouts held right in Cape Breton.

People living on Sydney Road in Reserve Mines became accustomed to seeing seemingly endless processions of headlights as hundreds of cars would pass by their homes heading to the old Miners Forum in Glace Bay. Thousands of people would crowd smoke-filled hockey rinks around Industrial Cape Breton, excitedly waiting for the sound of the bell. Allie Steele, among others, attributed the Cape Breton boxing craze to a culmination of three things. First, the war had recently ended, providing a ready source of boxers, as many of the fighters had boxed while in service; second, Johnny Nemis was on the scene and was willing to train many of the young men who wanted to continue in boxing after the war; and third, there was a very able promoter on the scene, a gentleman by the name of Gussie MacLellan.

MacLellan, a rather diminutive man known for his sharp clothes and love of cigars, had fought around the same time as Nemis and had also trained with him. MacLellan won the Maritime Amateur Lightweight Championship before he was sixteen and was considered one of the top fighters of his day. Steele describes MacLellan as a fiery, intelligent man who had just the right personality for boxing promotion. "He was well known, well connected, and he made his business to have the connections he needed to promote fights," said Steele. "So much had hinged on him, you know. He had boxing contacts in Halifax with a fellow named Brown. They did matches at the Halifax Forum. He knew people all over the States, too, and that was how he was able to put together some really, really good shows."

At the time, it took considerable money to bring fighters in to challenge the local boxers and to keep boxing contacts going. "Gussie wasn't afraid to put the money into the promotion to get it," said Steele. Indeed, it was a fact: MacLellan had the contacts, knew the fighters, and had all the information he needed to put together successful cards.

MacLellan ran a grocery store on the Esplanade in Sydney for many years, which was close to where the old Venetian Gardens was. The Gardens was the site of many matches over the years. The Venetian Gardens was built in the late 1940s by Florindo Byron, an Italian emigrant to Cape Breton who came from a village near Venice. The building was four stories high from the back and one and a half from the front. It sported a round roof and a large painting of Venice, complete with gondolas and canals graced the wall in the large dance hall. Dances, concerts, bingo and eventually

Fig. 1.7. Gussie MacLellan and Kid Hart. 1932. Clipping courtesy Tyrone Gardiner.

BEFORE BOXING BATTLE
1932

Gussie McLellan won the Eastern Canadian featherweight title when he outpointed the veteran Kid Hart of Moncton in a rugged battle. The above picture was taken as they weighed in, and shows, left to right Maurice MacDonald, promoter and former fighter, MacLellan, Stevie "Kid" MacDonald, former titleholder and manager of MacLellan, Manager Shea and Kid Hart, both of Moncton.

large boxing cards were staged at the Venetian Gardens. In *Italian Lives, Cape Breton Memories,* former boxer Benny DeLorenzo said, "I got involved with Mr. Byron to put on a few boxing bouts there (Venetian Gardens). I got a boxing ring made at the steel plant, and we set it up in the basement. We had the boxing matches downstairs, and the dances upstairs."[10]

Not far from the Gardens, up on Charlotte Street, MacLellan also ran the Press Club, a private club and bar frequented by local business people, especially employees of local media outlets such as the *Cape Breton Post*, as well as the sporting crowd at large. Years later he ran the Ceilidh Lounge at the old Isle Royale Hotel.

Steele explained that even if you have a great promoter in the area, you needed to have the local fighters because people weren't going to go pay to see out-of-towners fight. "But right around 1946 and 1947, in that period it just sort of meshed," said Steele. "You had a lot of guys. Some of them from Sydney, some were from Glace Bay and New Waterford. Plus you had Gussie and Johnny Nemis. Cape Breton was a real hubbub of boxing."

Steele said that, at the time, George Ross probably would have been the main headliner, though there were a lot of other good fighters around. "Everybody knows or has heard of George 'Rockabye' Ross," said Steele. "That seemed to be the catalyst that really got boxing going in the forties, and the momentum gained from that kept it going for a long time."

Allie Steele himself was boxing in the 1950s and early 1960s and explains how the boxers then were still benefiting from what had started after the Second World War. There were five boxing clubs going at the time, which was quite a bit for a small community when you consider the population.

 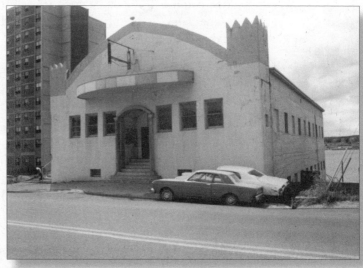

Fig. 1.8. Florindo Byron. Photographer unknown, Courtesy Gordon McVicar.
Fig. 1.9. Venetian Gardens. N.d.. Courtesy Gordon McVicar.

"I guess we used to have more wars in the gyms, in training. It was highly competitive and it sort of carried on," said Steele.

Steele recounted his first encounter with Johnny Nemis when he was seventeen. "I boxed from when I was fourteen or fifteen and I didn't have that many fights but I did win a number of them. I was away for a while and when I came back and I really wanted to get into it but I knew I had to get a good trainer." Steele didn't know anything about Johnny Nemis at the time so he did some checking around and discovered people were promoting fights down at the Venetian Gardens. Steele remembers the meeting.

"The place was packed. It would hold 400 people, and they'd have 500 in there. Smoke all over the place. Johnny was upstairs on the main floor getting a couple of his fighters ready, so I went up to him and said, 'Mr.. Nemis, I'd like to box. And I'd like you to train me.' And you'd have to know Johnny, he answered 'Yeah, well, you think you can fight?' I said, 'Well, we'll have to find out, but I'd like to try.' He said, 'Well, it's going to cost you $2.50 a night to train.' I said, 'Okay. I don't mind that.' 'Okay,' he said, 'next Monday evening you come in and I'll have a look at ya'."

Steele remembers that first Monday night when he went back to see Johnny Nemis. "I worked out, trained, and then took my $2.50 to him and he said, 'No. I don't charge *you* anything. You stay here, you're gonna be my fighter.' So it never even cost me the $2.50, you know!"

Allie Steele figured Nemis must have seen something in him that maybe even he himself hadn't been aware of, because he was such a good trainer and a pro and he could spot talent in a fighter. That's why he refused to make Steele pay to train with him. At that time Nemis was training his young fighters in the basement of the Venetian Gardens on the Esplanade in Sydney. "They had a good ring in there, and a heavy bag, but it was cold and damp," remembers Steele. "Everybody was dedicated to the sport back then."

"I saw fights in there between Gordie MacDougall and Bobby Moore. You know, they were two middleweights, and they could both fight like the devil. Gordie was really, really good. He was a great athlete, and he could run, play ball, anything. But, boy, they'd get in there in the gym for training and for three rounds they'd just hammer themselves. That's the way we were in training."

Gordie MacDougall credits Johnny Nemis with changing his life. As a youngster, MacDougall was often fighting, getting into trouble and being picked up by the police or the Mounties. Eventually the police introduced MacDougall to Nemis in an effort to turn him around. Nemis told MacDougall, "What I teach you in here, it's in here and that's as far as it goes. I don't want to catch you or the cops ever tell me that you used this stuff on the street, and if you do, you're out of this gym and don't you come back."[11]

In Nemis's gym the young fighters worked hard to hone their skills. According to Steele, "It was like you were in an actual fight and that's what you had to do. You can't pitter-patter around and then expect to win and not know how to fight off the ropes, you know. How to slip and slide a punch, or take a punch and counter and all that. I mean, you've got to be throwing some punches. You don't try to kill a guy, but you got to have some authority in your punches."

Some of the best fighters of this period started out in the dark, damp basement of the Venetian Gardens training with Johnny Nemis. "I'd be there probably four nights a week," said Steele. "We'd start at seven o'clock and go right on through the night with different guys coming in throughout the evening. Tyrone Gardiner used to work out with us there. Bobby Moore, Gordie MacDougall, and Allan MacKinnon from South Bar. They were all here at that time!"

By the 1960s, Johnny Nemis had earned the moniker "trainer of champions" amongst the local and more widespread boxing community. Over three decades Johnny trained Tyrone Gardiner, who went on to become Canadian Lightweight Champion, Gussie "Greased Lighting" McGibbon, Maritime Featherweight Champ, and a host of other great Cape Breton fighters such as Gordie MacDougall, Joe Pyle, Ike Gillis, Les Gillis, Archie "Bear" Hannigan and brothers Tony and Johnny Odo.[12]

In a 1964 article in *Punching with Pemberton*, Johnny Odo said his interest in boxing came from visits to the training quarters of Nemis and Buddie Lewis, also of New Waterford. "I gathered a lot of knowledge just by watching these two working in the gym, also by sparring with Nemis," Odo explained.

According to Odo there was never a shortage of opponents or sparring partners in the 1930s. "There were more good fighters around than you could shake a stick at. The fellow living next door would jump over the fence and give you a few hard rounds." Odo also had his younger brother "Tony Bulldog" to spar with.

The one-time ne'er-do-well Gordie MacDougall credits Nemis for keeping him on the straight and narrow. "The guy had a good impact on me. I just stuck strictly

Fig. 1.10. Champ Hannigan vs. Bobby Moore; referee Pordena Smith. Venetian Gardens. July 16, 1955. Abbass Studios Collection, Beaton Institute, Cape Breton University, 7970.

to boxing. I was dedicated to it. No one ever taught me more than Johnny Nemis did about boxing." Though he was an excellent trainer, MacDougall claims Nemis was a bad manager in the sense that money didn't matter that much to him. "Johnny fought in the twenties and thirties. He fought for wristwatches and suits of clothes, twenty, thirty dollars and maybe a meal. In those days when I could be getting $1000, $200 was okay. You know, you fight your guts out for $200. Then you're back two weeks later again for maybe $100. But it just rolled off."

One of Nemis's top boxers in the later years was Blair Richardson, who started off his career training with Nemis in 1955 and eventually went on to become, with subsequent trainers, Canadian and British Empire Middleweight Champion. In a 1964 article in the *Cape Breton Post*, Richardson was quoted as saying he still retained all that Johnny had taught him during his training days and early fights.

By 1964, Johnny Nemis had had enough of training in other people's gyms so he built one himself in the basement of his New Waterford home. He had a ten foot concrete room built under his home and then constructed a gym area measuring 38 feet by 28 feet with a nine and a half foot ceiling.[13] He outfitted it with all the latest in training equipment as well as pieces of equipment that he'd been using since the 1930s. Sally Durando recalls her Uncle Johnny had the best of everything in his gym. "He had no money but he was able to still get the best stuff; speed bags, punching bags, training gloves, boxing gloves, shoes, everything. I even remember as a little girl going down there to the corner where his house was and lacing on a pair of gloves. All the young guys were down there. He trained a lot of fighters. Plus he kept a horse and wagon and had a little garden as well."[14]

Fig. 1.11. Johnny Nemis and Blair Richardson. Abbass Studios Collection, Beaton Institute, Cape Breton University, A-6153.

Looking back today on the life and times of Johnny Nemis and the legacy of boxing greats he helped train and shape over nearly forty years, it's clear he played a pivotal role in the heyday of Cape Breton boxing. Many of his contemporaries felt that Nemis was never given his proper due. Johnny had a "special knack for teaching" according to referee Bucky Samson and others, but he also had an abrasive side that rubbed some people in boxing circles the wrong way. But first and foremost, Johnny Nemis cared about his fighters and what was best for

them. Many say that Nemis's greatest hope for a champion in his later years was Ernie MacKinnon of South Bar. A Cape Breton native, MacKinnon was considered to be a top contender for a Canadian championship. Tragically, MacKinnon died young, killed in a car accident, leaving his destiny as a fighter unrealized.

In a 1974 *Cape Breton Post* article following Nemis's own death, John Campbell wrote that the car accident that claimed MacKinnon's life was, for Nemis, "a tragedy that took a lot of the joy out of the boxing game for the veteran trainer from that point on." Though in ailing health in his final years, Johnny Nemis, according to Campbell, "never lost interest in the game that was, in effect, his life's work."[15]

Johnny Nemis passed away in September, 1974, in Camp Hill Hospital in Halifax at the age of sixty-nine. According to Sally Durando he suffered from Parkinson's disease in the last years of his life and his sister Eta took care of him at home in New Waterford. He ended up dying in the same city in which he briefly spent time some fifty years earlier as a young man getting his first taste of boxing by the Christian Brothers. Reflecting on Johnny's role as a boxing icon in Cape Breton, Campbell wrote that when he had asked Nemis for an interview one time, Nemis told him to "wait till I'm dead, than you won't have to tell any lies."[16]

Johnny Nemis was a complex and crucial character in the world of Cape Breton boxing. For many who remember those days, boxing wouldn't have become what it did without the contributions of Nemis and a handful of other key individuals. Nemis worked as a miner until 1948 when he took on training more or less full time. He also was an accomplished accordion and piano player who learned to read music at a young age. According to Sally Durando he was the only one of the eight Nemis children that was interested in music.[17] He used to play for his own enjoyment as well as at weddings and dances at the Italian hall in Dominion. He never married nor had any children, but was a favourite uncle to many of his sibling's children. Though most of his grand nieces and nephews barely know of his exploits in and alongside the ring, those that do know of him, know of him as both character and myth.

FATALLY INJURED — Ernie MacKinnon of Low Point, C.B., rated one of the leading contenders for the Maritime welterweight boxing title, died yesterday morning in New Waterford General Hospital from injuries sustained in a car accident Thursday night. MacKinnon, 19-year-old graduate of Xavier Junior College, had won 19 fights as an amateur. (For details, please see page 11)

Fig. 1.12. Ernie MacKinnon (death notice). *Cape Breton Post*. Clipping courtesy Tyrone Gardiner.

ROUND TWO
GEORGE "ROCKABYE" ROSS

In 1922, the year that Johnny Nemis, in his first professional fight, put Norman Elcock to the mat in New Waterford in the fourth round, George Ross was born at Marble Mountain, Inverness County. At the age of five, his family moved to neighbouring West Bay. George Ross's 11-year career in professional boxing spanned three continents, broke post-war attendance records, and led him to the Canadian Middleweight Championship in 1948.[1]

Ross's rise to the height of boxing in the late 1940s was nothing short of legendary and he was one of the major catalysts in the Cape Breton boxing scene until his retirement from the ring in 1957. Many consider Ross to be one of the greatest Canadian athletes of his day and he still remains an inspiration to Canadian boxing enthusiasts. At age twenty, Ross won a three-round decision in his first amateur match, fought against a sailor in 1942 at the Merchant Seaman's club in Sydney; just three years later, in 1945, he was the Golden Gloves Welterweight Champ of Cape Breton. His first professional fight was at the Kentville Arena in April of 1946, under the watchful eye of manager-trainer Johnny Odo of New Waterford. Referee Bucky Sampson had to call the fight in the second round after Ross put Haligonian Gordon MacNeil to

Fig. 2.1. George "Rockabye" Ross. Photographer unknown. Courtesy Tyrone Gardiner.

Fig. 2.2. (Below) Courtesy Karl Marsh.

the mat four times running. Seven quick knockouts later, a Cape Breton legend was born. Ross earned his nickname, "Rockabye," early in his career when he knocked out eight men in his first twenty-three rounds of boxing. In other words, his opponents lasted, on average, less than three rounds per fight. Rockabye indeed. Whitney Pier native and boxing hero in his own right, Gordon "Gramps" Kiley, claims Ross was so strong in those early days that he could "punch a hole in a concrete wall."[2]

Within six months, Ross had fought eight fights, which led him to his first ten-rounder versus Jimmie Pettie of Boston. Pettie was no challenge for Ross and his 4,000 fans packed inside the Glace Bay Miners Forum. Just seventeen days after his decision over Pettie, Rockabye fought again, putting Montrealer Ruby Margolin down in the sixth before a capacity crowd at the Halifax Arena. In 1947, Ross had seven fights, winning one by a knockout and six by decision. One of his biggest victories of that year came in October over Tommy "Gun" Spencer of New Waterford, who was the Maritime Welterweight Champion at the time.

Thomas Scott Spencer was born in 1923 (one year after Ross) and lived his early years in one of the roughest parts of the town of New Waterford. It was not uncommon for he and his friends to have to fight their way through the neighbourhood as they walked to and from their homes. At the age of ten, Tommy Spencer witnessed his first boxing match. It must have inspired him, for not long after that he donned a pair of oversized sneakers stuffed with newspapers and a baggy pair of trunks held up with a rope and a safety pin and entered the ring.

Spencer loved boxing and was hooked from the moment he started. Later in life he would reminisce about his boxing career with his two grown daughters, telling them how he'd loved every moment of it. "I loved the training and all the hard work I had to put into it," he'd tell them. "There was nothing else like it."[3] And there truly was nothing like it, as Spencer's training regimen was a Spartan affair that entailed rising at 4:30 a.m., having a quick meal of tea and toast, before heading off into the pre-dawn darkness to run nine miles along the local railroad tracks and then back into town. When he got home from his run, Spencer would eat a larger, heartier breakfast and then engage in a full day of backbreaking labour in the

Fig. 2.3. Tommy "Gun" Spencer and Al Hogan both fought George Ross. 1955. Abbass Studios Collection, Beaton Institute, Cape Breton University, 7621b.

New Waterford coal mines. After work, he'd hit the gym for another long workout that would stretch well into evening. The next day, he'd do it all over again.

In 1947, Spencer had recently returned to Cape Breton after battling his way through a number of bouts in the United States. Earlier in the year he had beaten fellow New Waterforder Joe Pyle, which would move him into the number two spot in the rankings for the Canadian Boxing Federation's welterweight division.

Though Spencer was an established pro at the time of his fight with Ross, he simply couldn't stop the hard-hitting boy from the West Bay Road. Ross was given the decision following ten tough rounds. Spencer declared himself "all washed up" with boxing after losing to Ross. Many insiders at the time felt Spencer may have gone into the fight a little overconfident. Ross rounded out 1947 with two more victories, defeating Billy Napper of Boston and Alvin Upshaw of Truro.

In early 1948, Ross took his battles south of the border to Hartford, Connecticut, and to Providence, Rhode Island, winning seven more fights in a row. By April of 1948, almost two years to the day that Rockabye had begun his professional boxing career, he had won twenty-four straight fights. In the annals of boxing history this is one of the greatest accomplishments anyone has ever achieved. Fighting on average one pro bout per month and winning all of them—with more than half the wins by knockout—is an astounding feat. To ask this of professional boxers today would be unheard of, though for boxers of the time it was considered routine.

While Ross's star was rising in the United States, back home in Cape Breton promoter Gussie MacLellan was busy at work setting up a title bout for the 24-year-old slugger. Hamilton native Len Wadsworth, a 31-year-old veteran known for a nasty left hook, was the reigning Canadian Middleweight Champion. The dapper MacLellan was able to convince Wadsworth and his team to fight Ross at the Glace Bay Miners Forum. On the night of May 1, 1948, more than 5,000 fight-crazy fans stormed into the Miners Forum to watch their hometown boy put it to the champ from Ontario. The match drew the largest indoor fight crowd in Cape Breton boxing history up to that time.

In the early stages of the fight, Ross was able to get inside on Wadsworth, all the while managing to evade the champ's mighty left hook. From early on, Wadsworth looked clumsy as the young challenger unleashed a seemingly unending barrage of body blows. By the seventh round, busted up inside, Wadsworth began to tire noticeably. Though he'd stood toe-to-toe with Ross through most of the fight, he was never able to hurt him. The eighth, ninth and tenth were furious rounds as Ross poured it on, determined to take the crown for himself. And over the final two rounds, the champ had no answer.

The final bell sounded and the crowd went wild. They, as much as Ross, wanted this national championship for themselves.

When Moody Allen, the ring announcer, proclaimed Rockabye Ross the new Canadian Middleweight Champion, the ovation was deafening as fans piled into the ring to pay homage to their new hero. The forum police had to be called in to clear the ring and make a path to the victor's dressing room. In the other dressing room, Wadsworth, ever the class act, declared Ross was tops as a fighter and as a man. "I'm not happy about losing," he said, "but I couldn't lose to a better guy."

Fig. 2.4. George "Rockabye" Ross (left) vs Len Wadsworth, title fight in Halifax, 1948. Photographer unknown. Courtesy Leo MacDonald and www.boxrec.com.

Gramps Kiley remembers Ross as one of the fighters he admired the most. "George was a gentleman in every way."[4] Kiley recalls one night early in both their careers when a boxer failed to show up for a match against Ross. As a big favour, promoter Gussie MacLellan asked the obviously unprepared Kiley to go up against Ross to at least "put on a show." "So we sparred four rounds," says Kiley. "George could knock your head off but he wouldn't do that, he just wasn't that kind of guy."

While Ross was taking the middleweight title from Wadsworth, Joe Pyle was making a run at the Canadian Welterweight crown. Pyle was born in 1923 in New Waterford.[5] His father MacDonald was from Barbados and his mother Eliza was from France. Joe was an all around athlete who played hockey, basketball and rugby. He served in the army and after his return he turned to boxing as his main sport. By 1949 most observers of the fight game considered Pyle to be the top boxer in Cape Breton, though Ross's meteoric rise had already begun to put this in dispute. While a number of Black families lived in Industrial Cape Breton in the 1940s, and many of their young men were involved in boxing, none achieved the level of success inside the ring as that attained by "Joltin" Joe Pyle.

Fight fan Charlie Hopkins of Sydney remembers that one of the more memorable boxing matches held in Cape Breton was between Joe Pyle and "Silent" Jim Anest. Anest was a boxer from New Jersey who was deaf and couldn't speak.[6] He was brought to Sydney by Constantine "Cus" D'Amato. D'Amato, as both trainer and manager, would become a boxing legend. In 1956, he led Floyd Patterson to the world heavyweight title,

Fig. 2.5. Joe Pyle.
Courtesy Karl Marsh.

making Patterson, at the tender age of 21, the youngest heavyweight champ in history up to that time. When the record for youngest champion fell, thirty years later, it fell to yet another D'Amato protégé—twenty-year-old Mike Tyson, who knocked out Trevor Berbick, a Jamaican who began his professional career fighting out of Halifax and Montreal, for the WBC heavyweight crown. That D'Amato was bringing his fighters from New York and New Jersey to Cape Breton speaks volumes about how Sydney and the surrounding area had become a boxing hotbed.

The Pyle vs. Anest fight was held at the Sydney Sports Center, which was the local horseracing track. According to Hopkins, occasionally a ring would be set up at the racetrack. "They would fight outdoors, and there'd be a couple of thousand people who'd go up there for a fight, especially if it was good weather." Of Anest, Hopkins noted that "his corner man would tap on the canvas and Anest would get the vibrations through his feet to let him know the bell had rung. Anest was quite the fighter." However, Pyle won the fight.[7]

On May 24, 1948, Joe Pyle was scheduled to fight Joey Peralta, a Mexican-American from Arizona with over a hundred bouts to his credit. Peralta had recently defeated Dave "Golden Boy" Andrews, a top New England welterweight and a fighter who'd knocked out Pyle a few months earlier in a fight in Massachusetts. Pyle's fight plans soon changed, however, when he was offered a chance to take on Vancouver's Phil Palmer, one of the leading contenders for the Canadian Welterweight Championship. Pyle won an easy decision over Palmer in mid-May but was in no shape to take on Peralta just one week later. Rockabye Ross, who'd already been in training, accepted an offer to fill in for Pyle against Peralta. So just twenty-three days after going twelve rounds with Len Wadsworth for the middleweight crown, Rockabye Ross returned to the Glace Bay Miners Forum for a non-title fight bout against the cagey veteran, Joey Peralta. From almost the first round, however, it quickly became evident that the Arizonian would be no match for the Canadian middleweight champ. Ross out-punched Peralta by five to one and took eight out of ten rounds for a convincing win by unanimous decision.

Though Tommy "Gun" Spencer's 1947 loss to George Ross had dampened his spirits for the fight game, he soon found that his mood had changed. He returned to training and had some heavy (and successful) workout sessions at the Strand Gym in New Waterford, sparring with Tony Odo. Feeling renewed, Spencer even went so far as to declare that if he were to fight Rockabye Ross again, and Ross was left standing after this second match, even his own mother wouldn't recognize him. George Ross readily accepted Spencer's challenge and the rematch, though not a title bout, was held on June 11, which is Davis Day in Industrial Cape Breton communities. Davis Day commemorates the death of pumpman and roadmaker Bill Davis, who was shot by the Coal Company police in 1925 during the miners' protests against the British Empire Coal Company. But in 1948, 4,000 Cape Bretoners were thinking less of mining struggles and more of whom to cheer on when two local champs came up against each at the Miners Forum. Rockabye Ross was Canadian Middleweight Champ at the time, while Tommy "Gun" Spencer held the Maritime Welterweight crown.

Fig. 2.6. Rockabye Ross vs Joey Peralta. Courtesy Leo MacDonald and www.boxrec.com.

Early on, Spencer appeared sharp enough and strong enough to avenge his earlier loss to Ross, but then he took a hard left hook to the right eye, which began to bleed profusely. Despite the cut, Spencer went punch for punch with Ross into the third and fourth rounds but soon began to falter. For every punch Spencer managed to land, Ross responded with a flurry of combinations to the body. By the eighth round it became clear to all in attendance that Spencer was tiring, and could no longer stay out of the way of Ross's devastating left fist.

Ross completed his brace of fights against Spencer by soundly winning the decision. The referee and two judges each scored Ross as winning eight of the twelve rounds. Though Spencer retained his Maritime Welterweight title after losing to Ross, he eventually gave it up when he moved into the Montreal-Toronto fight scene, where he felt things were more active. After eleven years in the ring

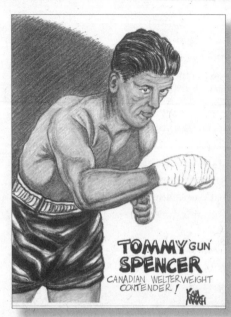

Fig. 2.7. Tommy "Gun" Spencer. Courtesy Karl Marsh.

Tommy "Gun" Spencer retired from boxing in 1954. He worked in New Waterford as a police officer for a number of years before moving to Toronto with his wife and children to take up a career in policing and security. His daughters Sharon and Laura remember him as a gentleman with a wry sense of humour who loved to dance.[8] He was "always impeccably dressed ... wore crisp white shirts with the cuffs rolled up and always sported newly shined shoes. He would walk for miles in his dress shoes...." Tommy "Gun" Spencer died in 2000.

A little more than a month after his second fight with Spencer, Ross put his title on the line yet again by taking on Roger Whynott of Mahone Bay, Nova Scotia. In the previous year, Whynott, known for a big left hook, had had won decisions over both Joe Pyle and Len Wadsworth and had been quickly making a name for himself. But alas, as was becoming all too common, Whynott's big left was no match for Rockabye's bigger one. Ross was the quicker puncher, too, and Whynott had difficulty avoiding the champ's vicious combinations. By the sixth round, Whynott realized he'd have to knock Ross out if he were to have any chance of winning the match. By the end of the fight, neither man had put the other to the mat but Whynott was much the worse for wear.

Fig. 2.8. Standing (left to right): Alderman Moriarty, unidentified, Alderman Lang, Alderman Buyess and promoter Gussie MacLellan. Seated: Roger Whynott (left) and Rockabye Ross prior to a fight between the two. 1962. *Cape Breton Post*. Clipping courtesy Tyrone Gardine

Sporting two nearly closed eyes, one with a bad cut over it, Whynott lost by unanimous decision.

The ever-astute promoter Gussie MacLellan realized after Rockabye Ross's victories over Spencer and Whynott that the best future gate receipts would come with a rematch against Len Wadsworth. Just a scant twenty-eight days after the Whynott fight, MacLellan arranged for Ross to defend his title at the Halifax Forum against the man he took it from a few months before. Wadsworth, though taller and heavier and with a longer reach, found that his natural physical endowments brought him no advantage over the smaller, faster and harder hitting Ross. The champ won, but it was close, with just a couple of rounds tilting the bout in Ross's favour. Ross went so far as to admit that it had been one of his tougher go-arounds in the ring. After the fight he was heard to say, "It was a tough fight. I don't know how I could have gone another couple of rounds."

Though Ross was punching his way through some of the finest boxers in Nova Scotia and New England, he hadn't yet come up against "Joltin" Joe Pyle of New Waterford. Many fight fans at the time were not yet convinced that Ross was the top boxer in Cape Breton, even though he was the reigning Canadian Middleweight champ. Not least among them was Joe Pyle himself.

Finally, the two heavy hitters crossed paths. Breaking all gate receipt records at the time, fight fans crammed into the Glace Bay Miners Forum on Labour Day, 1948, to see who would lay claim to the unofficial title of best boxing Cape Bretoner. Unfortunately, the fight itself, despite the anticipation and hype, was something of a disappointment. Pyle did connect with his much vaunted right a few times, but failed to inflict much damage on the champ, and for the thousands of fans in attendance the match was less than spectacular, more a show of defence on the part of both fighters rather than offence. And while the bout went the distance, Rockabye Ross took the win with a convincing unanimous decision. For Ross, the win over Pyle was his thirtieth in a row, in a little over two years.

Keeping with the tradition of staging fights on holidays, Ross's next fight was set for Thanksgiving Day against Pete Zaduk of Guelph, Ontario, who at twenty years of age was four years younger than Ross. Sports crazy Cape Bretoners were anxious for a good fight because baseball season was over and hockey had more than a month to go before it got into full swing. Zaduk, described in the press as the "baby-faced killer," was known for his right hand and was considered the favorite by some insiders, including Tommy "Gun" Spencer. By the second round of the non-title fight, which is now recognized as one of the legendary battles in Cape Breton boxing history, Zaduk put Ross to the floor with a devastating right uppercut that would have finished a lesser opponent. Fans were stunned, left to wonder if the farm boy from West Bay would make it up off the mat. With Ross down,

Fig. 2.9 and 2.10. George Ross (right) vs. Joe Pyle 1948 or 49. Photographer unknown. Courtesy Leo MacDonald and www.boxrec.com.

his head spinning, Zaduk accidentally headed for Ross's corner instead of a neutral one. This could have either disqualified Zaduk from the match or given the referee the option to restart the count on Ross. Zaduk's manager, Sam Keller, screamed at Zaduk to go to a neutral corner before the referee saw him and some believe it was Keller's screaming that actually jolted Ross off the mat at the count of six. Rockabye was able to pull himself from the mat and continue, but after the fight he claimed that he couldn't remember anything from the third round except thinking about being home on the farm. The announcer at first told the screaming crowd that Zaduk had won the fight because when the points were added up it came out fourteen to ten in favour of Zaduk. But since the judges were split on the decision, and referee Wilf Clements had it as a tie, the fight was ruled a draw. For Ross it was a bittersweet moment, he hadn't lost the fight, but for the first time in his career he hadn't won either. It was also the first time he had been knocked down. The up-and-comer Zaduk said afterwards, "Ross was the hardest puncher I ever faced in the ring."

Former boxer Allie Steele, who witnessed the historic Zaduk-Ross match, recalled it as one of the best fights he had ever seen.[9] "It was a hell of a fight. Ross was the old pro, while Pete Zaduk was the young kid from Ontario. Ross was the big mother here, no one expected a twenty-year-old kid from Ontario to come here and beat him. Zaduk was a hell of a fighter. It was ruled a draw, but Zaduk definitely won the fight. He was some fighter."

In January of 1949, Gussie MacLellan arranged a rematch of Joe Pyle and Ross at the Halifax Armouries. Ross had three months off from his fight with Zaduk, and began 1949 by defeating Wilfredo Miro in Boston in early January. Back to his regular schedule of a fight almost every three weeks, Ross was ready and willing to give Pyle another go for his money. Ross was being trained at the time by the legendary Al Clemente of Medford, Massachusetts. Clemente worked out of the New Garden Gym in Boston and trained some of the best fighters of the day including Billy McCluskey, George Colton, Jerry Forte and his own nephew Tony Shucco, who fought against five different world champions in his career. According to Earle Pemberton, Clemente managed Ross in all his championship bouts. At the time of the Pyle-Ross rematch, Clemente was warning everyone that Rockabye was back and looking for a knockout over Joltin Joe.

In front of the packed crowd in Halifax, Pyle was in command of the fight in the first two rounds. Early into the third many in the crowd were wondering if Pyle wasn't going to walk away with the Canadian Middleweight Championship. Pyle had slammed Ross with a devastating right cross, followed by another right and a left hook. Ross was visibly weakened as he worked his way off the ropes and tried to get away from the challenger. Pyle continued the onslaught, forcing Ross to strike out from a crouch. Pyle's attempt to put Ross to the mat failed, though, when he missed with a quick right and fell forward—right into Rockabye's big right fist. Ross recalls that the shock of hitting Pyle's chin directly sent vibrations up his arm and into his shoulder. With Pyle looking ready to fall, Ross pounded him with a left-right combination to the jaw. That was enough to knock Joltin Joe off his feet.

Al Clemente remarked later that Pyle was one of those fighters who "lose their senses completely when belted on the chin. Joe had absolutely no idea of the time or place when he got up after that crack on the jaw." Dazed and confused, Pyle was escorted limping to his corner by the referee after

 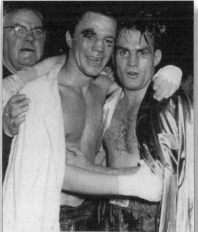

Fig. 2.11. George Ross (left) vs. Pete Zaduck. Glace Bay 1948 or 49. Photographer unknown. Courtesy Leo MacDonald and www.boxrec.com.
Fig. 2.12. George Ross (right) and Pete Zaduck after a draw. Glace Bay 1948. Photographer unknown. Courtesy Leo MacDonald and www.boxrec.com.

he failed to make the count. Despite the shaky start, in one amazing flurry of three quick, opportunistic punches, Ross retained his title with a third-round knockout.

After the fight, a knock came on the locker room door. Cutman Rudy Plichie states that Gussie MacLellan told him it was the manager of the Armouries, telling him no more fights with Ross could be scheduled there. The reason given? Overcrowding. Ross had such a charismatic appeal to the crowds everywhere he went that people flocked to see him. MacLellan had recognized this when he first saw Ross fight in Sydney's Venetian Gardens. According to Plichie, MacLellan often said no one had "it" like George Ross did.[10] In his later years, MacLellan said he was glad there was no television in Ross's day because with his thick Scottish accent, no one would have understood him in an interview, though those closest to him say he'd have been too modest to give one anyway.

Over the next two months, Ross fought two more fights in Boston, winning both by decision, before giving the kid from Ontario, Pete Zaduk, a second chance to take him on. This time it was for the title. Zaduk's manager, Sam Keller, was convinced Ross was going down this time because he felt that Zaduk had got the better of him in the first match, only to have it called a draw because, in Keller's view, Ross was the hometown favourite. This time, Keller was sure it would be a decisive victory for his boy Zaduk. 4,500 fans jammed into the Halifax Forum in May of 1949. The fight had been postponed a week to allow Zaduk to recover from a cut over his left eye. Gussie MacLellan was more than happy to agree to the postponement. He didn't want anyone to claim afterward that the challenger wasn't given every opportunity to be ready for the fight. Clearly, Zaduk was ready, going the distance with the champ but, at the end of twelve rounds, Ross was awarded the victory with a unanimous decision. As was so often the case with George "Rockabye" Ross, even his adversaries had kind and respectful words when it came time to describe their experiences with him. As Keller himself admitted after the fight, "George was a lot sharper than he was in Glace Bay. And a fine boy. A good clean fighter. A real gentleman."

Though Ross had soundly beat Zaduk, the young Ontarian wasn't finished tackling Cape Bretoners. His next match put him up against Joe Pyle. Pyle is quoted as saying "the chips are down. I want another bout with George Ross. Zaduk will be the stepping stone." Zaduk and his team felt otherwise though, as did the "smart" money in Halifax. Most bets were on Zaduk to put the New Waterforder to the mat. It took the full ten rounds, but Joltin Joe showed a full house in the Glace Bay Miners Forum that he still had his spark and was still a contender. He won an easy decision over the young Ontario puncher. But more important, the win set him up for a third shot at Rockabye Ross.

On June 20, 1949, Joe Pyle squared off against George Ross for the third time within nine months. More than 5,000 fans packed the Miners Forum once again to cheer on the two local boys. Pyle was on the move most of the fight and, to many observers, was the more aggressive of the two, particularly early on. In the third round he was especially aggressive, nailing Ross with a hard left that opened an old cut above his eye. The cut never stopped bleeding and by the seventh round both fighters were blood-soaked. Respectful of the champ's punching power, Pyle attempted to connect with punches from outside, but for the most part Ross was able to dodge them and so was never really hurt by Pyle. Ross, on the other hand, took the fight inside to Pyle's body, and wouldn't be deterred. Though Pyle was still standing at the end of twelve rounds, Ross was awarded a unanimous decision. It had become obvious that the New Waterforder, while game enough, was out of his league with Rockabye Ross. It was now doubtful that Pyle would ever defeat the champ. Joltin Joe retired the following year with forty-nine fights under his belt, including thirty victories.

After the Pyle slugfest Ross didn't fight for the next couple of months in an effort to allow his cut eyebrow to heal. Compared to the schedule he was used to, it must have felt like an eternity waiting for his next bout. In today's boxing world fighters routinely stay out of the ring for a year; and to take a few months off for an injury to heal is also commonplace. In the hardscrabble forties though, that kind of time away from the ring was seen as a major layoff.

In August of 1949, Ross embarked on the next stage of his boxing career. He and Gussie MacLellan went to England for what was to be a seven week stint to arrange a title match with the British Middleweight Champion Dick Turpin. Whether he believed it or not, Ross said he felt his eye was healed enough to take on anyone that came his way. The Turpin fight wasn't as easy to arrange as the savvy MacLellan may have expected. When they arrived in England, MacLellan, to his great chagrin, was informed that Roy Wouters, the Western Canadian Middleweight Champion, was also on the Isle looking for a fight against Turpin. By late August, neither Canadian slugger had a match arranged with Turpin or anyone else.

To make things worse for the anxious Ross, a match had been arranged between Turpin and an Australian named Dave Sands for 6 September. Sands finished off Turpin in dramatic fashion—a first round knockout. This set the stage for Sands to take on the winner of an upcoming match between world champion, Jake LaMotta, and Marcel Cerdan of France. The Turpin fight was sidelined for the time being.

Fig. 2.13. Newspaper advertisement for Ross vs. Pyle. Clipping courtesy Gordon Kiley.

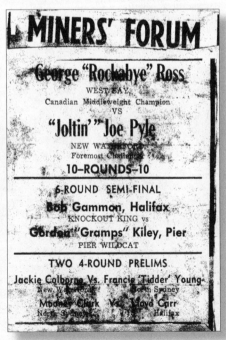

MINERS' FORUM

George "Rockabye" Ross
WEST BAY
Canadian Middleweight Champion
VS
"Joltin'" Joe Pyle
NEW WATERFORD
Foremost Challenger

10—ROUNDS—10

6-ROUND SEMI-FINAL

Bob Gammon, Halifax
KNOCKOUT KING vs
Gordon "Gramps" Kiley, Pier
PIER WILDCAT

TWO 4-ROUND PRELIMS

Jackie Colborne Vs. Francie 'Tidder' Young
New Waterford   North Sydney
Mooney Clark Vs Lloyd Carr
North Sydney   Halifax

Other problems plagued Ross's quest for a fight in England as time went on. Squabbling between English promoters was forcing an elimination match between Wouters and Ross for the right to meet Sands in an Empire title match. Wouter's promoter was a bit more successful than MacLellan and was able to match his fighter against Randolph Turpin, Dick's brother and a serious contender in his own right, for a September 19 bout. Turpin knocked out Wouters in the fifth.

A few days before Wouters lost to Turpin, MacLellan signed Ross to a ten-round match against Albert Finch, a contender for the British Empire Middleweight Crown, and a fighter who'd easily defeated Randolph Turpin earlier that year. If Ross could put away Finch, it would clear a path to Dave Sands or even to Marcel Cerdan. Ross began training at the Crown and Anchor Gym in Brighton, England, with world bantamweight champ Manual Ortiz as a sparing partner. On October 4, more than 9,000 fans packed the Empress Stadium at Earl's Court in London to watch an undefeated farm boy from West Bay, Cape Breton, take on one of England's finest middleweights.

What should have been a glorious day for George Ross and his legion of fans home in Cape Breton and throughout much of Canada turned into disappointment as Ross's much maligned eyebrow began to bleed in the very first round. Nevertheless, the two men hammered away at each other, with Ross almost putting Finch down in the fourth round. By the ninth round, things were even on most judges' scorecards but a combination of Ross's inability to see through the blood that seeped from the cut above his eye and a terrific rally by Finch in the tenth decided the match. Ross suffered his first defeat, far away from home in a foreign country with nothing to show for it but a bloodied head and a battered body.

Around the time of the Ross-Finch bout, Dick Turpin's promoter was looking for someone to take on his boy. Antonio Soldevilla, the Spanish Middleweight champ, had just pulled out of a match against Turpin, leaving him with no one to fight. When Ross entered the ring against Turpin on November 1, less than a month after his loss to Finch, he had plaster above and below his left eye. The plaster was an unwanted souvenir from Finch—and a red flag to Turpin.

Fig. 2.14. (Left to right) Gussie MacLellan, Albert Finch, unknown, Rockabye Ross, unknown, in England. Courtesy Leo MacDonald and www.boxrec.com.

As expected, Turpin opened the cut early and continued to target it throughout the fight. Though observers say Ross was likely ahead of Turpin on points, the cut and the blood made things too difficult for Ross. In the seventh round, he did manage to connect with a right that clearly staggered Turpin, but he got a stiff jab to the eye in return. So much blood was streaming down Ross's face that mid-way through the seventh the referee called the match. It was Ross's second defeat on English soil in less that a month. By now, Rockabye Ross had had enough of Old Blighty.

In retrospect, some say Gussie MacLellan may have been too quick to match the injured and beaten Ross against the British champ. Although, to be fair to MacLellan, it was in all likelihood a case of "take it now or lose the chance." Veteran boxer Allie Steele felt that Ross should never have taken the fight against Dick Turpin, and that his loss to Turpin was the crucial "point of no return" in his career. While he was forced to return home from England defeated, Ross's fate was ultimately more fortunate than some of the other fighters who were in Europe at the same time as himself and Roy Wouters.

Dave Sands never got his chance to take on the winner of the LaMotta-Cerdan fight because Cerdan was killed in an plane crash in the Azores, along with his manager and trainer, on October 27, 1949. They had been on their way to the United States to fight LaMotta. Not long after Cerdan's tragic end, Sands himself died in a car crash in Australia in 1952. Meanwhile, LaMotta would be immortalized as one of the great legends of boxing in the 1980 film *Raging Bull*, directed by Martin Scorsese.)

Though Ross had suffered defeat at the hands of two highly capable fighters in England, many boxing scholars agree that it was the cut above his eye, which was never given enough time to properly heal, plus the hazardous amount of scar tissue from having had the cut reopened so many times, that led to Ross's defeat. Add to this the fact that the pressures of maintaining such a heavy fight schedule took a heavy toll on the West Bay puncher. Even so, Ross was still the undisputed Middleweight Champion of Canada when he returned to Cape Breton in November, 1949, and the fight the English promoters had wanted to see on their home turf, that of Ross versus Wouters, was in the making.

When Wouters returned to Canada he was quickly matched up to fight the colorful, and undefeated, Yvon Durelle. In a little over two years the young Durelle had punched his way through nineteen opponents, knocking out half of them in less than two full rounds. Durelle was born in 1929 in a remote New Brunswick fishing village and was considered a formidable opponent by anyone involved in the fight game in his home province. Not only would Wouters be the first opponent to make Durelle go the distance, he would also be the first man to defeat Durelle in a career that lasted sixteen years.

Rockabye Ross was reading about Durelle's loss to Wouters while he was chopping wood in a lumber camp in Ontario. Gussie MacLellan was at work making the calls from his home in Cape Breton to make the fight with Wouters a reality. Sure enough, in March, MacLellan announced Ross would fight Wouters for the Canadian Middleweight Championship in an April, 1950, twelve-rounder. The challenger is reported as saying he would have such a commanding lead in points, "I won't have to worry about a hometown decision. When you're far enough ahead you don't have to worry about judges." The only thing that worried the Ross camp was that his cuts would reopen, bleed and obscure his vision.

As it turned out, the eye didn't play a major factor in the fight. When the bell sounded to signal the start of the fight, Ross came out looking sharp enough, and while his left jab seemed to be working, he quickly began to tire—and it showed. The 4,500 fans in attendance began to sense the inevitable. Wouters landed a right to Ross's jaw in the fourth that Wouters later claimed was the clinching blow. "He was never the same after that," Wouters said from his dressing room after the fight. And sure enough, it was mostly downhill for Ross from that point on. He took a nine count in the seventh; followed by a tough eighth round; and hit the deck again in the ninth. Ross's manager, Al Clemente, fearing further damage to his fighter, threw in the towel. Roy Wouters of Vancouver was now the middleweight champ of Canada.

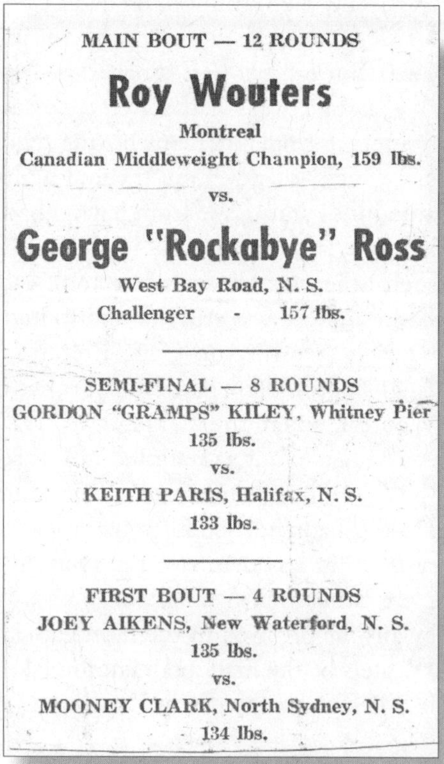

Fig. 2.15. Fight program from Ross vs. Wouters. Courtesy Gordon Kiley.

After the fight, the usually taciturn Ross stated that he had never met such a powerful fighter as Wouters, and "for the first time in my life I fought a man stronger than myself." Wouters himself was so impressed with Ross that he gave him a rematch. Wouters fought one non-title bout before he faced Ross for the second time on Dominion Day, 1950, in Glace Bay. More than four thousand people showed up, making the Ross-Wouters rematch one of the biggest draws in Cape Breton boxing history. And the fighters delivered. For the first eight rounds, the crowd got their money's worth. Both men tore into each other with sharp, quick uppercuts and heavy, punishing right hands to the

---

MAIN BOUT — 12 ROUNDS

Roy Wouters
Montreal
Canadian Middleweight Champion, 159 lbs.

vs.

George "Rockabye" Ross
West Bay Road, N. S.
Challenger - 157 lbs.

SEMI-FINAL — 8 ROUNDS
GORDON "GRAMPS" KILEY, Whitney Pier
135 lbs.
vs.
KEITH PARIS, Halifax, N. S.
133 lbs.

FIRST BOUT — 4 ROUNDS
JOEY AIKENS, New Waterford, N. S.
135 lbs.
vs.
MOONEY CLARK, North Sydney, N. S.
134 lbs.

body. In the eleventh round, Wouters proved he was worthy of the crown by pounding Ross with a series of devastating combinations. Ross answered the bell in the twelfth but couldn't muster the knockout punch he needed to wrest the throne back from the western king. The decision was unanimous, but close, with all three judges awarding Wouters seven of twelve rounds. Roy Wouters went on to fight Yvon Durelle a second time in January, 1951, and won. He then retired from the ring, leaving the Canadian Middleweight Championship vacant.

Ross went into semi-retirement after his second loss to Roy Wouters, but in October of 1951 he travelled to Washington and Oregon and won six victories in three months. In September, 1952, he beat Glace Bay's Al Hogan in Glace Bay in ten rounds and then defeated Eddie Zastre in a ten-rounder in North Sydney. Ross was back in the game again and the title vacated by Roy Wouters the previous year was still unclaimed. In what Ross would later declare as the toughest battle of his ring career, Yvon Durelle came to Cape Breton to fight Ross for the undisputed Middleweight Championship of Canada.

Fig. 2.16. (Left) Newspaper advertisement for Ross vs. Wouters. Clipping courtesy Gordon Kiley.

Fig. 2.17. (Below) George Ross vs. Al Hogan. North Sydney, 1952. Photographer unknown. Courtesy Leo MacDonald and www.boxrec.com.

BOXING

GLACE BAY FORUM
Labor Day Night

1st Bout 8.30

MAIN BOUT - 10 ROUNDS

GEORGE ROSS
162
WEST BAY

vs.

AL HOGAN
172
TORONTO

Semi-Final - 8 Rounds	6 Rounds
ARNOLD FLEIGHER 159 Chatham, N. B.	**GORDON KILEY** 140 Sydney, N. S.
vs.	vs.
FREDDIE WILSON 165 New Glasgow, N. S.	**DON TRAINOR** 142 Charlottetown, P. E. I.

Admission: Ringside $2.50 Reserved $2.00 Rush $1.25

TICKETS ON SALE AT THE FOLLOWING PLACES: Sydney: Diana Sweets and Sport Mart. New Waterford: Medical Hall and Rexall Drug Store. Glace Bay: Bob MacKenzie's Barber Shop and Clarence MacLellan's Barber Shop. North Sydney: Bud McDonald.

Fig. 2.18. Poster promoting Ross vs. Hogan. Courtesy Gordon Kiley.

ROUND THREE:
YVON DURELLE COMES TO TOWN

After winning eight straight fights since his Canada Day loss to Roy Wouters in 1951, Rockabye Ross was back. He wanted to regain the Middleweight Championship and he was ready to take on any serious contenders for it. After staging such a dramatic comeback, Ross was ranked second behind Yvon Durelle of New Brunswick. The Canadian Boxing Federation had sanctioned the fight as a championship bout for the crown left vacant by Roy Wouters's retirement. Durelle was in Picton, Ontario at an army training camp when Gussie MacLellan approached Dode Dealy about setting up a fight. Dealy was a former fighter, a referee, a bit of a promoter and one of the original organizers of the Chatham Athletic Association, a group that is credited with popularizing boxing in New Brunswick in the years following the Second World War. Dealy, however, was afraid that Durelle was taking it too easy in Ontario and putting on the beef, therefore taking himself out of contention for a middleweight fight. Durelle felt otherwise, though. He assured Dealy he could get down to the proper weight by the day of the fight.

Fig. 3.1. Yvon Durelle in Sydney. 1958. Abbass Studios Collection, Beaton Institute, Cape Breton University, A-3251.

Durelle had arranged for a boxing leave from the army and arrived in New Brunswick a week before he was to travel to Glace Bay to fight Ross.[1] Everyone was so confident Ross would beat Durelle that they already had him booked to fight in Australia once he'd disposed of the New Brunswicker. When Durelle met up with Dealy he was so fat and out of shape that Dealy barely recognized him. At 203 pounds, Durelle was 43 pounds over the maximum weight for a middleweight and with a week to go before the fight.

Johnny Nemis, who was training Ross at the time, got wind of the excess baggage that Durelle carried back from Ontario and was soon on the phone to Dealy voicing his concerns. Nemis emphasized that if the fight didn't go off then Ross would most likely have a good claim on the title without having to throw a punch to get it. Though titles are sometimes decided this way these days, to become a champion by default in the 1950s was not considered proper. Nemis wasn't interested in training fighters that didn't earn their rewards. Fans and fighters would both be cheated out of what they wanted, a clear-cut victory over a worthy opponent. Nothing less would do.

The first thing Dealy did in his rigorous, no time to spare, weight loss regimen for Durelle was to load him up with heavy sweatshirts and get him to try running some of the lard off at the Chatham racetrack. Durelle dropped a couple of pounds but Dealy realized it wasn't going to get him down to fight weight in time. A more original weight loss program was needed. Dealy figured that if he put Durelle in the drying kiln at a local lumber yard he just may be able to sweat him down to 160 pounds. The kiln was normally used to steam wet lumber to force the moisture out of it. As a cure for obesity, however, it was untested.

The first day in the kiln, Dealy had Durelle stay inside for ten minutes. The trainer claimed the fat was pouring off of Durelle like butter. He took the fighter off all liquids and starchy foods and made him do a little exercise. On the second day Durelle spent fifteen minutes in the kiln, and after getting weighed he was down about ten pounds. Quite an impressive weight loss by today's standards. With four days to go Durelle had thirty more pounds to melt off. The next two days Dealy had Durelle take two shifts in the kiln and by the last two days before heading to Glace Bay, Durelle was hitting the steam bath three times a day. The day before the fight Durelle was sitting in the lumber kiln at seven o'clock in the morning, sweating himself down to the required fight weight. Dealy wrapped him in some blankets and put him in the back seat of the car for the long drive to Sydney. Durelle slept like a baby most of the time waking only occasionally to guzzle down bottles of pop. They made it to Sydney later that afternoon and booked into the Isle Royale Hotel, which was located just down the road from the Venetian Gardens. The Isle Royale was the largest hotel in the city at the time and the bar downstairs was the haunt of choice for Sydney's fight fans, promoters and hangers-on. Gussie MacLellan ran the downstairs bar for a number of years. The hotel even had its own steam bath, and this was where Durelle spent part of the evening. Future Canadian lightweight champ Tyrone Gardiner observed that Durelle even steamed off the last of his excess weight at a lumber kiln in Sydney that evening, as well.[2]

First thing on the morning of May 2, 1953, Gussie MacLellan appeared at the hotel with a set of bathroom scales. Durelle weighed exactly 160 pounds. MacLellan was impressed. Dealy wouldn't let Durelle eat anything solid until the official weigh-in later that afternoon. The official scale read 159.5 pounds. Durelle immediately headed for the restaurant and had a steak. The burly New Brunswicker had made it and, minus some 43 pounds, was ready to fight. As usual, over 5,000 delirious fight fans showed up in Glace Bay that night at the Miners Forum. With the return of their hero

Rockabye Ross, the fans were cheering for a homegrown victory. Durelle had already made a reputation for himself as a scrapper and a worthy opponent but that didn't dampen the spirits of the local crowd—Rockabye Ross was back and they were behind him.

For the first four rounds, the match was close. Normally a slugger, Durelle was showing some moves that night that surprised even Dealy. Durelle gave Ross a few good shots in the fifth, but Ross recovered quickly. Ross decided to take the fight inside and pounded Durelle's ribs and stomach. But the onslaught of body blows didn't seem to slow the New Brunswicker down. Even the loss of forty pounds had no obvious effect on Durelle's famous ability to absorb a punch. As the fight wore on it began to become apparent that Durelle was going to outlast the once unbeatable boy from West Bay—and in the ninth round, Durelle sent Ross to the mat. For the next three rounds, Durelle continued the assault until, in the twelfth and final round, the fight was stopped. Durelle was victorious. The next morning, with his $2,800 winner's purse in a paper bag tied with a piece of string, Durelle headed with Dealy back to New Brunswick, having effectively sent Rockabye Ross back into retirement.

A short time after the loss to Durelle, Ross began working for a company setting up a power line from the Seaboard power plant in Glace Bay to the Sydney steel plant. Unfortunately, Ross suffered his greatest injury a few months later when he fell forty-five feet from a power pole in Reserve Mines. He was laid up for six months with injuries that might have killed a man of lesser physical stature. Upon recovery, Ross decided to move to New Zealand to cut timber, his fighting days apparently over.

One can only speculate on what would have happened to Rockabye Ross if his eye injuries and rigorous fight schedule hadn't conspired against him. It has certainly been observed that, had he been given adequate time to heal, the two fights in England may well have turned out different. While the two losses in England did little to help Ross prepare for his subsequent battles against Roy Wouters, one could argue that Ross was officially done for after the second defeat at the hands of Wouters. The rally in 1951 may have put him back in the winner's circle, but losing to Durelle, who had to be nearly steamed to death to make weight, was the final straw. Ross would later go on to say that his fight against Durelle was the toughest of his career. Later that year, Durelle won the Canadian Light Heavyweight title by defeating Gordon Wallace in a twelve-round decision held at the Sydney Forum. He lost the title to Doug Harper two months later in Calgary, only to win it back from Harper in July of 1954. In September, 1954, Durelle was paired up with Gordon Wallace once again in a title defense. Wallace failed to regain the title, losing the decision after twelve hard fought rounds. Durelle went on to fight twenty-one more fights until he met up with Wallace one last time in 1957. This time he knocked Wallace out in the second round to claim the British Empire Light Heavyweight title. All that was left to conquer after this fight was the world crown.

By 1958, Yvon Durelle had already secured for himself a place in Canadian boxing history. But a couple of weeks before Christmas, Durelle was to meet his greatest opponent yet. In what many recall as a great fight, Yvon Durelle went toe to toe with the great Archie Moore for the Light Heavyweight Championship of the world. The fight took place in Montreal and today it's still regarded as one of the legendary boxing matches in the annals of Canadian and world boxing history. To deafening roars from the Montreal crowd, Durelle got off to an auspicious start, knocking the champion to the canvas three times in the first round, and once more in the fifth. Moore eventually won the fight, but it took him eleven rounds to finally knock Durelle out. Years later, the always colourful Durelle would tell Sydney boxer and Canadian Armed Forces Middleweight Champion Eddie McKillop that he had "made more money in a crap game than in that fight with Archie Moore."[3]

Durelle fought Moore again in Montreal eight months later but was knocked out in the third round. In 1959, Durelle fought the great George Chuvalo in Toronto for the Canadian Heavyweight title. Chuvalo, of course, is best remembered for his 15-round war with Muhammad Ali, which would come a few years later, in 1966, and prompt the battered but victorious Ali to proclaim Canada's own Chuvalo as "the toughest guy I ever fought." Durelle lost to Chuvalo, but it was another close one, a knockout in the twelfth and final round. Durelle only fought three more bouts after that and by 1963 had retired from the ring for good. He eventually opened a bar, called The Fisherman's Club, in the little village of Baie Ste. Anne, New Brunswick.

Fig. 3.2. (Left to right): Yvon Durelle, unidentified, Willie Williams and Gussie MacLellan. 1958. Abbass Studios Collection, Beaton Institute, Cape Breton University, A-3251a.

Around midnight on May 20, 1977, a former friend of Durelle's named Albin Poirier entered Durelle's club. Poirier had a troubled past which included attacking another barkeeper, serving time in jail for assault, and attempting a rather grisly suicide by tearing into his own stomach, exposing parts of internal organs. His mental health was highly suspect and he'd spent time in and out of mental facilities in New Brunswick. Most of his time outside one form of lockup or another found him preoccupied with bootlegging and generally making people feel uneasy. On numerous occasions Durelle had to escort Poirier out of his club. This night things would go bad. Durelle had been calling the RCMP all day asking them to deal with Poirier, because Poirier was calling making threats against Durelle if he didn't close his club down and move away. The police didn't consider the threats that serious, figuring if Durelle couldn't handle some noisy drunk then who could?

Durelle met Poirier at the door when he entered and quickly escorted him outside and stuffed him into his car. Witnesses outside the club stated afterward that Poirier started his car and gunned it towards Durelle. Fearing for his life, Durelle took out a handgun and shot at the car. It should be noted that guns and barkeepers were a common thing in rural New Brunswick at the time. Poirier smashed into another car as Durelle ran over to the car and unloaded four more bullets through the window, stopping Poirier and his menacing ways for good. Poirier's reasons for his hostility towards Durelle remain with the deceased. Durelle was charged with second-degree murder and ordered away from The Fisherman's Club while he was on bail. The trial started on September 12 and lasted a week. Fortunately for Durelle, the jury found him not guilty. He remained a free man. The young defence lawyer who handled most of the courtroom proceedings was Frank McKenna, who went on to become one of the most successful and popular premiers of the Province of New Brunswick.

Yvon Durelle died in New Brunswick in 2006. Former CJCB radio sports director Dave LeBlanc remembers meeting Durelle years after his fighting days in Cape Breton. "Yvon Durelle had to have had the biggest hands of anybody I'd ever seen," related LeBlanc. "He wore a size sixteen ring. Do you realize how big that is? He had big, big fingers. He was *so close* to beating Archie Moore for the world championship."[4]

A month after Yvon Durelle won the British Empire Light Heavyweight title in1957, Cape Bretoners were surprised to learn that the man who put Durelle on his winning path was making a return on the other side of the world. Rockabye Ross, away from the ring for more than four years, had begun training again in Australia. A match was arranged for Ross to fight Peter Bothe, a native of Austria who had just recently turned pro in Australia, winning his first nine fights, eight of them by knock-out. A huge crowd showed up at Wollongong Stadium on July 19, 1957, to see the veteran Canadian

Fig. 3.3. (Left to right): Carmen Basilio, Earle Walls, Yvon Durelle, unknown and Rubin "Hurricane" Carter at a Hall of Fame dinner. Oromocto, NB, 1987. Courtesy Eddie McKillop.

slugger take on the younger, up and coming Austrian. Bothe proved a cagey opponent for Ross, taking it on the chin numerous times but still coming back swinging. Though Ross staggered Bothe in the eighth round, Bothe was able to avoid Ross's deadly knockout punch. In the end, the ten-round decision went to the Austrian, even though he collapsed after the bell and had to nurse injured ribs for six weeks afterward. Encouraged by his performance against Bothe, Ross agreed to another fight on Australian soil that same year. This time it was against a native Australian. Harry Castles had won thirty-eight of his forty-one fights, though he wasn't considered the favourite in this match. Ross fought hard and did indeed prove that Castles was no match for him. Ross won the decision in what was to be his last professional boxing match. Castles went on to fight and beat Peter Bothe six months later by dropping him to the canvas in the ninth round.

Longing for home, George "Rockabye" Ross returned to Cape Breton shortly after his victory over Harry Castles in 1957. Upon returning home he applied for a boxing licence from the Cape Breton, Halifax and New Brunswick boxing commissions respectively, but was refused by all, mostly for reasons of health relating to the scar tissue around Rockabye's vulnerable eyes. While not by his own choosing, and for the sake of his continued good health, Ross's meteoric career had finally come to an end. Ross died in 1997; he never married or had children. Of the class act that was George "Rockabye" Ross, Al Clemente once remarked to a group of sportsman that "George Ross is the kind of fighter that bobs up only once in a century."

Was Clemente right?

ROUND FOUR: STILL MOVIN'
GRAMPS KILEY, HILTON SMITH & EDDIE MCKILLOP.

In 2004, at the age of 75, Gordon Kiley—"Gramps" to his friends—looks the same as he did back in 1948 when he first got interested in the fight game.[1] Gramps weighed in at 133 lbs back then, and today he's no more than 140. He's led what he calls "a clean life," with no smoking or drinking and plenty of physical activity to keep him in the shape he was in when he first took an interest in boxing.

"In 1948, when I was just fifteen years old, I went to the Golden Gloves boxing tournament. It was for Cape Breton Island and all the fighters used to enter it. Guys from Glace Bay, New Waterford, North Sydney, Sydney and the Pier all had teams. There were different weight classes and many people would be crowned Golden Gloves champions by the end of the tournament. Seeing the guys fight in 1948 made me want to get involved and it wasn't soon after that I started going to the gym and hanging out with the other boxers of the day which included Benny Delorenzo, Hilton Smith, and Mitch Krszwda, among others."

Kiley was the oldest boy in a family of sixteen who lived on Muggah Street in Sydney's Whitney Pier district. His parents were from Newfoundland, which was still, when Kiley was born, a foreign country to Canada. As a young boy, Kiley had to help support his family because his

Fig. 4.1. Gramps Kiley. Photographer unknown. Courtesy Gordon Kiley.

father took sick very young in life. Kiley acquired the moniker Gramps at an early age because he always looked and acted older then he was. He worked at a local bakery for a while before making the switch to the steel plant. "Dad used to say to me, 'don't go to that steel plant.' When I got there I loved it, the work and everything, but I found out why he didn't want me to go there. He worked in one of the worst places you could ever work in, the bundling shed. They used to bundle bails of wire and he worked there and that was hard work." Kiley only lasted a few shifts in the bundling shed before getting moved into the blast furnace. In 1950, Kiley was already training with Bucky

Fig. 4.2. Benny Delorenzo and Gordon "Gramps" Kiley. Clipping courtesy Gordon Kiley.

IN MARITIME MITT TOURNEY—Benny DeLorenzo, 124, of Sydney, won the Maritime Amateur Featherweight boxing championship at Moncton last night while Gordon Kiley, 133, won the runner-up position in the lightweight class.

Sampson at his gym located in the basement of the Steelworkers Hall on Prince Street in Sydney. It was Sampson who helped get Kiley moved into the blast furnace. The blast furnace at the Sydney steel plant had to be one of the hottest and most dangerous places on earth at the time, but for Kiley it was a godsend. "I loved working in the blast furnace. I worked there for fifteen years before getting my electrical papers and then I spent twenty years as an electrician at the plant. Working in the blast furnace was so physical it kept me in shape for boxing."

In the heyday of Cape Breton boxing it was not unusual for men to get up and run long miles before going to work in the coal mines or the steel plant. Many then trained in the evenings in the local gyms and boxing clubs, and would run again at night, too. Gramps Kiley personified this style of training. He would often run three miles through the Pier from his home to Inglis Lake and then return to work a long shift in the grueling heat of the blast furnace. He'd then look after things at home and later on train in the gym with Sampson, Arkie Dalton, Frank and Tom Stricky, and Eddie Bosch. There was no shortage of places to train in the 1940s and 50s in the Sydney area. Kiley trained at the Venetian Gardens on the Esplanade and the Lyceum on George Street as well as at the CCF Hall and the Imperial Hall in Whitney Pier. "Anytime you wanted to go spar against some different guys it was easy to arrange, because there were so many clubs and gyms around that time," recalls Kiley. "There were a few priests involved in boxing back then, too."[2]

While many people today believe that boxing has evolved into a brutal spectacle that's more about money than athleticism, it was quite a different thing in post-war Cape Breton. For one thing, boxing was viewed as a way to keep people on the straight and narrow, and many young men wanted to be involved in it. At the time, boxing was as popular as hockey, basketball and soccer are today. While for members of the clergy, boxing was an honourable way for them to help young men that may have been veering from what they, the clergy, considered to be the path of righteousness. Just as it is not uncommon to see clergy involved in hockey and other sports these days, they were similarly involved in boxing decades ago.

Fig. 4.3 Clipping courtesy Gordon Kiley.

Kiley recalls that he and others would occasionally venture from Sydney to go to boxing matches arranged by local area priests that had connections to other parishes in Nova Scotia. Father Power from the Pier had come from a parish in Guysborough County and Kiley would go there to spar with some of the local boys. Father Mickie Malcolm MacDonald of Ingonish arranged for young Sydney men to go and tangle with some of the boxers north of Smokey. "I have a picture of me and three others from Sydney in Ingonish on the golf course," Kiley recalled. "We're holding golf clubs but not one of us was up there golfing. I can't remember who took the picture, but I guess it was to promote us going to Ingonish. I've never golfed a day in my life." According to Kiley, the trainers he had were all good fellows. "They wouldn't do anything to harm you and they made sure that you wouldn't be overmatched and they looked after you the best way they knew how. They were your friends. The fighters were all friends, too. There was never any animosity amongst us."

Fighters had to have discipline back then, recalled Kiley. "You wouldn't do any drinking or smoking. I started smoking but soon quit when I learned it wasn't good for me. I wanted to avoid anything that would interfere with my boxing and training. Boxing put you on the road to a healthy body and mind." Kiley said that in the eleven years he boxed, which

IN SEMI-FINAL CONTEST—Sydney's popular Gordon "Gramps" Kiley meets Til LeBlanc of Shediac, now fighting out of Moncton, in the six-round semi-final to the Hannigan-Durelle Maritime lightheavyweight title match at Glace Bay Forum, Saturday night. Promoter Gussie MacLellan said last night that Kiley, who is handled by Bucky Sampson, was going through a strenuous training grind and would be in top condition for the Saturday go.

ended when he got married, he never felt he got injured in the ring. "Sure I got knocked down a couple of times, but I never got knocked out. I had thirty-five amateur fights and twenty-five pro fights and I finished every one of them. I lost ten out of the sixty fights, but the most important thing to me was to finish the fight. My biggest fear was not losing a fight, but not finishing one, especially getting stopped in the first round. I would consider it a disgrace if some guy came out and put your lights out in a few seconds. I didn't like to lose but if you lost there's nothing you can do about it. Train harder, see what you can do from there."

"There were a lot of great fighters around when I was boxing," says Kiley. "There was Tommy 'Gun' Spencer, who I sparred with. Joe Pyle and Red MacPherson were around and lots of other guys from the mines." MacPherson held the Light Heavyweight Championship for a time in the 1950s. "Mick Conway and Mitch Krszwda were rugged individuals, they could fight," says Kiley. "I sparred with Johnny Whitehouse, too. George Ross was around at that time also. George and I were friends. George used to work at the Arcade Grocery store, either the one on Charlotte Street or the one on the Esplanade. He used to deliver groceries for Gussie MacLellan, his promoter."

Cut man *extraordinaire* Rudy Plichie, who has been around boxing in Cape Breton as long as anyone can remember, describes Gramps Kiley as an incessantly aggressive boxer who was always in superb condition. "He was a throwback to the old days, when a fighter came to fight. He was blessed with stamina, and fought some of the best fighters in Canada during his career."[3]

One of Gramps's most memorable fights was against Keith Paris for the Maritime Welterweight Championship. Gramps had beaten Paris on four earlier occasions and felt he could take him for the title. The previous fights were hard fought battles but Paris wasn't able to outbox the Golden Gloves

Fig. 4.4. Fr. Mickie Malcom MacDonald and young fighters, Whitney Pier High School. Photo by H. Dodge Studio. Courtesy Whitney Pier Historical Society.

Gloves champ from Muggah Street. Gramps recalls that Paris had obtained one of the McCluskey brothers from Prince Edward Island to train him for the title match. "This trainer had seen me box before," said Kiley. "He knew more than the previous trainer and he knew he could tell Paris how to beat me. That's the tricks of the game, everyone can see something others can't see." McCluskey gave Paris enough of an advantage not to get beaten by Gramps, but not enough to secure a win. The match ended in a draw.

Fig. 4.5. Red MacPherson. Courtesy Karl Marsh.

Fig. 4.6. Poster promoting Gramps Kiley vs. Keith Paris. Courtesy Gordon Kiley.

Gramps Kiley is one of the most humble people you could ever meet and his quiet, reserved manner wouldn't make anyone think he was a force to be reckoned with in the boxing rings of fifty years ago. But according to Rudy Plichie, Kiley should have been a Canadian champion if he had had the right breaks. Sometimes it's more a case of fortune than anything else that puts you in the right ring at the right time with the right opponent battling for a title. Though he doesn't easily crack a smile, Kiley finds it humorous that today many people remember him for losing a fight to J. B. "Kid" Adshade. Adshade, who hailed from Glace Bay, was recognized as one of the

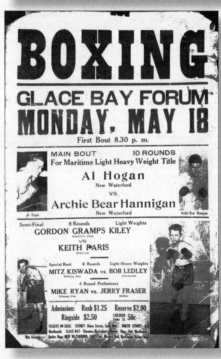

hardest punchers in his class. He had the record for the fastest knockout in Maritime boxing circles at the time; 41 seconds over Earl Trader of New York at the Miners Forum. "We were working our way to the Maritime Welterweight Championship when I fought Adshade," says Kiley. "I had beaten him before but no one remembers that. It was a good fight but he won. Next he went on to fight Tommy "Gun" Spencer. I really didn't think

Fig. 4.7 Poster promoting Gramps Kiley vs. Kid Adshade. Courtesy Gordon Kiley.

Fig. 4.8. (Right) Kiley in the ring with Kid Adshade, Glace Bay Forum; Kiley won by decision. Photo by Walker. Clipping courtesy Gordon Kiley.

BINGO!—Gordon "Gramps" Kiley, Sydney lightweight has just connected with a ri... to J. B. Adshade's jaw in the late rounds of a torrid, six-round semi-final on last nig... boxing card at the Glace Bay Forum. Kiley won the decision.   —Photo by Walke...

Adshade would beat Tommy Gun, but he did, and he won the crown for it."

After Kiley retired from the ring he spent a number of years as coach and referee. He's kept himself in great shape, too, just like when he was in his prime. Only these days, instead of running those miles every day, he walks them.

One of the first boxers Gramps Kiley encountered when he began training in 1948 was Hilton Smith from Whitney Pier. Smith been boxing a few years before Kiley with the encouragement of his father. Smith's father was a boxing fan and considered those involved in the sport to actually be rather gentle people. He thought if his young son Hilton got involved in boxing it would keep him away from fighting in the streets, something the senior Smith abhorred.

Hilton's father was a custom tailor who came from the West Indies. His mother was a Newfoundlander. The Smiths had seven children and over the years Hilton's father had three different tailor shops in Sydney. At age 78, Hilton Smith, like Gramps Kiley, weighs little more than he did back in the 1940s. He still runs every day and looks much younger than his years. He was not only a great athlete but is a perfect gentleman, too. Smith boxed from about the age of twelve to twenty. He moved to Toronto when he was twenty-four, after working for five years at the steel plant, and remained there for over thirty years working for the railroad. He moved back to Sydney after he retired. Though he was away from Cape Breton for most of the glory days of boxing, Smith remembers quite a bit about what it was like boxing there in the 1940s and 50s.[4]

When asked about his friend from fifty years ago, Gramps Kiley, he recalled how he used to call him Slow Motion Kiley because he was so quiet. "He fought the same way, too, he just walked straight ahead, he was tough, a brawler who could take a good punch. You'd have to take a punch or you couldn't be there. How long could you last? Some guys packed it in after one or two fights."

Boxers weren't the only tough people involved in boxing, either, according to Smith. The fans could dish it out just as good as any fighter, especially if you were coming into their hometown to take on their boy. Smith describes boxing out of town:

"You're alone in there. You have to have guts when you're fighting in the ring, especially if it's out of town, say in a place like New Waterford. You have to be on your toes. They don't want you to win. And the fans were tough. They just root and root for the other guy. Just like when those guys came to the Menelik Hall in the Pier. But it wasn't easy to fight away from your own hall. The Strand Gym in New Waterford was the toughest place to fight. Fans don't want to see you kissing a guy or holding hands in the ring. The fans back then were tougher than the fans that we have today."

Fig. 4.9. Hilton Smith (back row centre), with his parents and siblings. Courtesy Hilton Smith.

Smith began his early boxing days training at the Menelik Hall with Charlie Sheppard as his trainer. He also trained at other halls in the area including the Imperial Hall. As a young boxer in his early teens, Smith was daunted by the size of the crowds that would turn out to see amateur fights staged at various halls in the Pier. "For a young kid to see three to four hundred people show up to watch you box was something. Watching young guys fight today I say to myself, 'Did I actually do this?'" Even when training, Smith recalls that the gyms were often crowded. Everybody that was into sports was into boxing as well. "Lots of kids played all the sports, baseball, hockey and others. The boxers were hockey players, too, but they'd never fight on the ice," he said.

Smith remembers watching guys like Tommy "Gun" Spencer and Joe Pyle in fights and in training. "Tommy Gun was a good friend of mine and one of the nicest guys you could ever meet," said Smith. "He was a precision fighter and a good dancer. Pyle and Tommy Gun were good friends and they'd box against each other. Joe Pyle could hit like a mule." Smith also remembers seeing Sugar Ray Mascoll fight and recalls that he was quite the boxer in his day. "Johnny Nemis trained a lot of good fighters back in his day

Fig. 4.10. Whitney Pier Athletic Club. Taken at the Seaman's Club. 1946. Clipping courtesy Hilton Smith.

as well. He was a firecracker, Nemis was."

Smith fought as an amateur in the Cape Breton circuit and also fought 25 fights with the army prior to his move to Toronto, going 15-5-5, and was the central command Middleweight Champion at one time. In his mid seventies he was running twelve miles four mornings per week to keep in shape. He was running on an average ten races per year. Running for him today has become somewhat akin to boxing. "It's still all about you yourself. Whether you're going into the ring or standing at the starting line, it's really all up to you. No one else can really help. You're all on your own," he says. In 2005, at the age of 75, Hilton Smith completed his first marathon.

Boxing in the military was quite commonplace when Hilton Smith was a young fighter in his prime. Eddie McKillop of Sydney was another fighter who went far in the boxing ranks during his time spent in the Canadian army.[5] McKillop got his start in the old Local 1064 Steelworkers Hall, as did many other fighters. McKillop said in 2007 that he remembers the first time he went into the Steelworkers gym in 1950 just like it was yesterday.

"Bud Greer and I were kicking around at the time and I knew Bud was fighting. We'd get together and he'd always be bugging me to 'come down to the gym, come to the gym.' It all pretty well started from there. I was 15 at the time. Gramps, Benny Delorenzo, Mitch Krszwda, Bud Greer, we all trained there. Bucky Sampson ran the whole show down at the gym. Mooney Clarke, Tyrone Gardiner, Tommy Gun, they all used to come in there quite often. Little Dick Howard from Halifax used to come and train whenever he was fighting here."

McKillop fought and won the Golden Gloves championship in his first fight at the Venetian Gardens. The circumstances that led up to the fight are an example of how easily a teenager in Cape Breton could become initiated into boxing.

"The Golden Gloves came up at that time and I fought Greg Hannigan. He was Archie 'Bear' Hannigan's brother. It was sort of funny in a way, how that first fight happened. I went down to the Venetian Gardens and was sitting in a car with this Campbell guy from Baddeck when Greg and Bear came by. Bear, who I didn't really know at the time, said 'He [Campbell] can't be fighting here tonight because he's fighting pro. He just knocked a guy out in the Miners Forum.' I never paid any attention to it and went into the Gardens. While we were getting all wrapped up they came around and asked if anyone wanted to fight Greg Hannigan. They asked Bud and he said 'Nooo.' I was a saucy kid at the time and wouldn't say no if someone was going to kill me so I said I'd fight him. It turned out he was southpaw but I won the decision anyway and that was my first fight."

Fig. 4.11. Hilton Smith, Petawawa, ON. 1958. Clipping courtesy Hilton Smith.

McKillop found out afterwards that none of the fighters in attendance that night thought he'd have a chance in his very first fight against Greg Hannigan. "When I came down the stairs after the fight Mitch Krszwda was there and he said, 'I thought you was going to get killed.' I said well thanks a lot. You didn't tell me any of this before the fight did you. My father was there that night and he didn't say too much about it, but my mother got wild when she found out about it."

For weeks after McKillop's initial foray into boxing he'd find trainer Bucky Sampson, Gramps Kiley and Mitch Krszwda waiting for him in his driveway. They were training to go to fight in New Brunswick and wanted McKillop to come along. He told them, "No, it's lucky I survived this thing, I'm not going." When they went to New Brunswick they took Bud Greer and he got a licking at the hands of the fighter McKillop was lined up to go against. "Bud wasn't a happy camper after that," said McKillop. "I didn't fight again until I got into the military."

A few months after McKillop's Venetian Gardens victory he joined the militia and spent most of the time away from Cape Breton, not boxing much at all. In 1954 he join-

Fig. 4.12. Eddie McKillop. Photographer unknown. Courtesy Eddie McKillop.

Fig. 4.13.
Greg Hannigan, New
Waterford. 1955. Abbass
Studios Collection, Beaton
Institute, Cape Breton
University, 9043.

ed the Canadian Forces and was off to Germany within a few months. It was here he donned the boxing gloves for a second time and quickly began to make his mark as a fighter to be reckoned with. McKillop fought consistently throughout his military career, which lasted until 1964. While boxing, he was also a teacher and conditioning coach for the Canadian Military team. He won the Canadian Forces Middleweight and Light Heavyweight Championships and in 1955 defeated Ed Heath, the British Army's champion. That same year, in Soviet-occupied East Germany, he knocked out its champion, Stu Muller.

McKillop was considered by many in the boxing world to be the best prospect the Canadian Forces had since the Second World War. McKillop was at the peak of his career in 1964 training for the upcoming Olympic Games in Tokyo. He was thought to have a good chance of bringing home a medal for Canada. Earlier that year he defeated Larry Cardinal who held the Forces Middleweight Crown for four years running and was also Canadian Middleweight Champion. McKillop recalls that in the 1960 Pan-American Games Cardinal was given the victory, but then lost in a recount by one point in a fight against Wilbur "Skeeter" MacClurey of Detroit. MacClurey went on to fight in the Rome Olympic Games that same year and was voted best fighter in the Olympics and became Middleweight Champion of the World. He was on the same American boxing team as Muhammad Ali. With the Cardinal victory under his belt, and to be in a league of recognized world champions, things couldn't have looked better for Eddie McKillop of Cape Breton, who was also sporting Captain's stripes in the military.

Unfortunately for McKillop, as well as for his fans at home on Cape Breton Island, forces conspired against his making it on the world stage— the Canadian Armed Forces, to be exact. All of his skill, talent and heart, couldn't overcome the bureaucracy that would prove to be McKillop's toughest opponent. A few months prior to the Olympics, a military boxer injured a civilian boxer and this lead to a review of boxing in the military. A complaint was made which ended up on the desk of an MP in Ottawa. As is often the case in Military matters, swift justice was meted out and the entire Canadian Forces boxing program was cancelled. No member of the military was allowed to go to the Rome Olympics. McKillop was devastated. He couldn't believe what the army had done to ruin Canada's chances at an Olympic medal. In a 2005 interview in the *Cape Breton Post*, when he was inducted into the Cape Breton Sports Hall of Fame, MacKillop explained how he felt about the situation some forty years ago.

"The best fighters were in the service at the time. It was a full-time program and we had the best of facilities. We had a lot of success and when they cancelled it a lot of people couldn't understand it. Unfortunately when the armed forces makes these foolish decisions, nothing much changes after that. I thought they were actually joking the day my boss called me in and said, 'No more fighting in the armed forces.' I said 'What? What the heck are the armed forces all about? Are they going to take our rifles away from us next?'"[6]

McKillop felt the decision to be so unjust it became one of the main reasons he left the Forces. He retired from boxing a few months later, in 1964, with an impressive record of 41-2. McKillop spent many years working in various countries throughout the world and eventually found his way back to Sydney. He married Loretta Boudreau and had two children Kip and Shauna Lee. Like his father, Kip is now a member of the Canadian Armed Forces.

McKillop was inducted into the Canadian Boxing Hall of fame in 1985, the Canadian Forces Hall of Fame in 1996, and the World Boxing Hall of Fame. MacKillop's 1963 Light Heavyweight Forces title, his 1964 Middleweight Forces title and subsequent victory over Larry Cardinal were the beginning of a rapid series of Cape Breton boxing feats that put the island and its skilled boxers in the middle of the national ring. For boxing in Cape Breton, it was a time of plenty.

Fig. 4.14.
Eddie McKillop, Armed Forces Middleweight Championship. (Left to right): unidentified armed forces general, opponent Larry Cardinal and McKillop. Photographer unknown. Courtesy Eddie McKillop.

Fig. 4.15.
Eddie McKillop with Reuben "Hurricane" Carter. Hall of fame event, Oromocto, NB. Photographer unknown. Courtesy Eddie McKillop.

ROUND FIVE:
TYRONE GARDINER, CHAMPION TIMES FOUR

Cape Breton's infatuation with boxing continued into the late 1950s and 60s because the young men who put the island on the world's boxing stage kept turning up in the gyms of various union halls, dance clubs and bingo parlors across Cape Breton. There was a constant overlap of enthusiastic fighters, sparring partners, trainers, good boxers and great ones cropping up everywhere. For every legendary Cape Breton boxer like Rockabye Ross there were dozens of other younger boxers, like Eddie McKillop, Hilton Smith and Gramps Kiley, slugging it out in the hopes of becoming the next champion, or at least getting the chance to engage in battle with one.

In her book *On Boxing*, a literary examination of the essence of boxing, the American writer Joyce Carol Oates states that baseball, football and basketball are recognizably sports because they involve play, they are games. Oates states, "One plays football, one doesn't play boxing."[1] Tom Henry, in his book *Inside Fighter*, echoes these sentiments when he states that "to rank fighters by victory only is to ignore their greatest triumph: being there."[2] In some ways, both writers are correct when one looks at the state of professional boxing today and how it got that way in the past thirty years. But in the late 1940s through to the 1960s, so many young men were involved in boxing that one could argue that—yes—it really was about play.

Many boxing scholars agree that George Ross was within a few punches of becoming a world champion. If things had gone better in England, if his damaged eyebrow had been allowed to heal, he may had gone further than he did. One can only surmise where Ross would have ended up. Ross was an exemplary fighter and he personified what hundreds of young men in Cape Breton strove for, which was to be the best that they could be through vigorous physical training, hard work in the coal mines, at the steel plant or in the woods, and, for the majority of them, living clean and healthy lives.

During the heyday of Cape Breton boxing, boxing was *the sport* of the time, with hundreds of young boys and men involved in one way or another, and thousands of fans attending fights. As champion upon champion from Cape Breton was crowned over the years, they all started out the same way: as young boys hanging out in the gyms watching the older fellows—one could say—at play.

In 1952, the year before Rockabye Ross meet his match in Yvon Durelle, thirteen-year-old Tyrone Gardiner, while walking home from Ashby School in Sydney, stopped to look in the basement window of the Steelworkers Union Hall located on Prince Street. There were a number of young guys inside training and working out. His interest was piqued and eventually he began dropping into the hall and watching the boxers train. Gramps Kiley was boxing out of Bucky Sampson's gym and training with him back then and the young Gardiner remembers hearing about Kiley's success in the ring and how he was one of the best boxers to come out of Sydney. Sampson, who'd trained many of the great Cape Breton boxers, asked the young Gardiner if he wanted to help out with the boys. Gardiner readily agreed and started by getting the boxers water and tying on gloves. He soon began punching on the heavy bag and before he knew it he was in the ring sparring with fighters his age. Gardiner recalls: "At first I was only catching punches to help the fighters. Bucky Sampson was very good to me and got me sparring with the fighters. He made sure that no one would hurt me."[3]

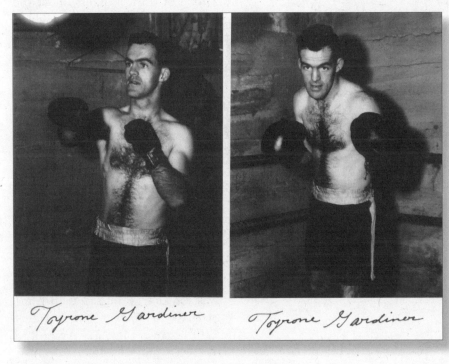

Fig. 5.1. Tyrone Gardiner training, Venetian Gardens. Photographer unknown. Courtesy Tyrone Gardiner.

In 1954, Bucky Sampson moved his gym from the basement of the Steelworkers Hall to Whitney Pier. Gardiner and some of his friends from the gym then moved to the Venetian Gardens located on the Esplanade in downtown Sydney. It was at the Venetian Gardens in a ring built at the steel plant that Tyrone Gardiner met the legendary Cape Breton boxer and trainer Johnny Nemis and his boxing career began.

Nemis had the remarkable ability to see potential in a young boxer and he never turned anyone away who was willing to do the work. Because Gardiner was so light, weighing only 113 pounds, Nemis gave him lots of time to practise in the ring before he put him into an actual bout. Lots of time to train in the 1950s in Cape Breton meant a few months, and by September of 1954 Gardiner was ready for his first match. Rather than fight amateur, Nemis felt the young puncher from Ashby was ready for the pros.

Fig. 5.2. A large sundial adorned the façade of the Venetian Gardens. Photo by Raytel. Clipping courtesy Gordon McVicar.

"What time is it by the sun?" will be a popular question in Cape Breton when the citizenry reverts to

His first fight was at the Venetian Gardens against Wally "Boom Boom" Gillis of Whitney Pier. Gillis only lasted two rounds before the young Gardiner knocked him out.

The following year, Gardiner fought and won six more fights. In 1956 he fought six more times, losing three and winning three. By the end of 1956, Gardiner had fought a total of thirteen fights under the guidance of Johnny Nemis. But in 1957 the young Gardiner decided training with Nemis wasn't right for him and decided to stop boxing. A year later he realized he still had the boxing bug in him and decided to team up with another well-known trainer, Johnny Cechetto. Gardiner's first fight under the direction of Cechetto was against Harold "Tobacco" Tonnery of New Waterford, in a bout staged at the Venetian Gardens. Gardiner and Tonnery slugged it out for three full rounds, but according to local newspaper reports Gardiner's timing was off and he missed with some of his best shots. Gardiner's first fight against the New Waterford southpaw ended in a draw. Gardiner fought twice more in 1959, winning both matches. In 1960, he started out the year with a draw against Kenny Dean, then lost his next three fights. The last loss was in the fourth round of a rematch against Tobacco Tonnery.

Talking to sportswriter and boxing scribe Earle Pemberton back in the 1960s, Gardiner said, "When I started with Mr. Cechetto, opponents were scarce and I had to fight men much heavier. After fighting Harold 'Tobacco' Tonnery in July 1960, Mr. Cechetto told me to quit fighting or I was going to get hurt, and that he wouldn't let me fight again unless I was going to train hard and show him that I was in top condition before each fight."[4] Unfazed by the knowledgeable trainer's stark forecast, Gardiner continued to train as hard as he could. Veteran cut man and boxing scholar Rudy Plichie describes Gardiner's stamina as coming from cutting pulpwood, roadwork and medicine ball sparring with bigger boxers rather than other lightweights. "He was capable of boxing ten and twelve rounds on short notice. His training methods were for endurance fights, like an old time pugilist."[5]

Fig. 5.3. Donnie Ferguson, John Cechetto and Tyrone Gardiner, Venetian Gardens. 1958. Abbass Studios Collection, Beaton Institute, Cape Breton University, A-3377a.

Gardiner fought Kenny Dean again in October of 1960, knocking him out in the third, and then went on to meet Sugar Ray Mascoll for the Nova Scotia Lightweight title. The night Gardiner faced off against Mascoll at the Venetian Gardens he weighed 135 pounds, and Mascoll was considerably heavier. The weight difference should have given Mascoll a major advantage but it was offset by the remarkable condition that Gardiner was in. Gardiner soon took command of the fight and won it in the fourth round. At the tender age of twenty-one, the young lad who got interested in boxing by peering in the basement window of the Steelworkers Hall was crowned Lightweight Champion of Nova Scotia. The first of four titles he never relinquished.

In 1961, Gardiner fought and won two fights before meeting George Munroe in Halifax for the Maritime Lightweight title. Gardiner won a six round unanimous decision, which set him up for a chance to fight for the Eastern Canadian Lightweight crown. Gardiner's opponent was LeRoy "Rocco" Jones. Jones was an experienced fighter at the time and had a number of ten-round fights under his belt. This match was to be Gardiner's first ten-round fight. According to Gardiner, the Jones fight was the only one in his career that he was frightened. And for good reason. Talk among the boxing crowd was that Jones was the type of fighter who knew all the tricks. He was known to use his glove laces, his elbows, and anything else to stop his opponent without letting the referee catch him in the act. In *Halifax Champion*, trainer Tom McCluskey describes Jones as an outright character that used to wear big white boots, was always in good shape and threw punches all over the ring. He'd, "throw junk here, throw junk there," recalled McCluskey.[6]

Gardiner had a host of other boxers from Cape Breton willing to help out and spar with him.[7] He credits John T. MacDonald, Les Gillis and Basil Arsenault with helping him win the Munroe fight. For the battle against Jones, BoBo Bonaparte, Ronnie Sampson and Roy Lewis were in his camp, as well. Gardiner said Jones "used every trick he knew and he knew plenty of them."[8] Up to that point it was one of the best fights in his career. Veteran sports writer Russ Doyle described the fight the next day in the *Cape Breton Post*.

"Gardiner weighing 134 lbs rocked and socked his way to the well-earned decision as he cocked the classy Halifax pugilist with stinging rights to the head and well placed lefts to the body. Gardiner displaying his best form took command of the feature event at the outset and after staving off a strong bid by Jones in the middle rounds came on to finish up in championship style. Although staggering his opponent on a number of occasions Gardiner was unable to apply the finishing touches as the more experienced Jones clinched at every opportunity. Jones showed his best form in the middle rounds when he caught Gardiner with a number of jaw jarring rights. The Halifax cutie scored well with both

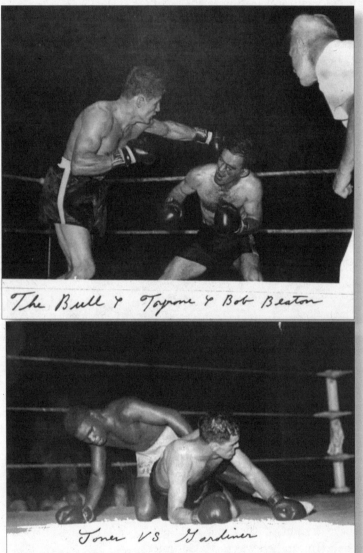

Fig. 5.4 Leroy "Rocco" Jones (left) vs. Tyrone Gardiner. Ca. 1964. Photographer unknown. Courtesy Tyrone Gardiner.

The Bull & Tyrone & Bob Beaton

Jones VS Gardiner

hands but Gardiner threw up a tight defense and threw Jones best shots off with his arms. Referee Pordena Smith warned Jones for low punching in the seventh round and again in the eighth."[9]

By the time the tenth round came about Gardiner had Jones holding on to him throughout the round. Gardiner proved his mettle against the notorious Jones winning the fight by a unanimous decision and capturing the Eastern Canadian Lightweight championship.

In keeping with the tradition of Rockabye Ross, Gardiner fought his next fight, after winning the Eastern Canadian crown, just three weeks later. His opponent was Rejean Robert of Montreal and Gardiner ranks this as one of the toughest fights he was ever in. The match was promoted as the first in a series of fights in which the winner would ultimately meet the Canadian title-holder, Lennie Sparkes of Halifax. Russ Doyle of the *Cape Breton Post* wrote, "Gardiner set a torrid pace in the early rounds of the fight as he battled Robert with digging lefts and rights to the head and body. Robert kept strictly on the defense in the bout fighting from a crouch, covering himself well and although taking a terrific amount of leather faired none the worse in the end."[10] Gardiner clearly remembers hitting Robert at will, but the Montreal fighter kept coming in. According to Gardiner, "After you pound a guy like that for a few rounds you sure get worried. To make it all the harder it went the full ten rounds." In the end, Gardiner won the unanimous decision over the indefatigable Rejean Robert.

In November of 1961, Gardiner suffered a setback in the Halifax Forum where he lost a six-round decision to Les Sprague of Amherst. Gardiner went on to fight and win seven bouts in the following year before running into Sprague again in August of 1962 at the Sydney Forum. The twelve-round match was for the Canadian Junior Welterweight Championship, left vacant when the Canadian Boxing Federation lifted it from Halifax's Lennie Sparkes earlier that year for failing to defend the title. Ian Donaldson described the bout in the *Cape Breton Post* the next day.

"Sprague, a hard punching blonde from Amherst sent Gardiner down for good after the Cape Bretoner struggled through the ropes after being knocked out of the ring. Referee Carmen Basilio, former world welterweight and middleweight champion, stopped the fight at 2:09 of the eighth. Sprague was ahead most of the way except for trouble in the first and fifth rounds, but the Sydney, NS, fighter stayed with the hard-hitting Sprague all the way."[11]

Sprague said after the fight he was amazed when Gardiner came back after taking an eight count outside the ring in the eighth. The Cape Bretoner was driven through the ropes landing on his back on a ringside table after Sprague scored with a series of hard left hooks and straight rights. Gardiner came back, took a token swing then caught a swinging right hook on the jaw. Basilio called the fight immediately.

One of the roughest fights Gardiner had that year was a match-up in Sydney against Rolly Thibault. "He [Thibault] bulled me and rushed me to the ropes at every opportunity. In one of the clinches he picked me up in a wrestling style crotch hold and slammed me to the floor. He could have been disqualified for his foul tactics, but I wanted to win fair and square," said Gardiner. And win he did. Gardiner took a unanimous decision over the less then gentlemanly Thibault.[12]

That same year, Gardiner tackled Bobby Speight of Saint John, New Brunswick twice, winning both fights in the third round. In the first match, staged at the Venetian Gardens, Gardiner defeated Speight by a technical knockout. The rematch occurred on the Dominion Day holiday at the Caledonia Hall in Grand Anse, Cape Breton. The *Cape Breton Post* described the short punishing fight the next day.

Fig. 5.5. Carmen Basilio (right) with Eddie McKillop. Oromocto, NB, hall of fame event. Photographer unknown. Courtesy Eddie McKillop.

"Gardiner opened fast and carried the fight to his opponent in the early stages. Gardiner got the better of a number of exchanges in the first round and then gained the margin in the second round. The third round opened fast with Gardiner constantly moving in and forcing his opponent to the ropes. Gardiner sent Speight to the canvas for a seven count early in the third round when he exploded with a sharp hook to the jaw."

"The Sydney River pugilist stalked his prey and seconds later pounced to the attack to again send him to the floor after an exchange at mid ring. Speight came around slowly this time and managed to beat the count. Gardiner again came to the fore and dealt severe blows to the head before Speight reeled to the canvas. Referee Smith then stepped in to signal the end."[13]

Gardiner credits part of his success in boxing to the fact that there were plenty of fights to be had. Heading into the 1960s, there were lots of opponents in all weight classes. Gardiner said, "You want to train much harder when you know that there is a fight coming soon." After beating Rolly Thibault in May, 1962, the 23 year-old triple lightweight titleholder felt he had only one thing left to prove to himself and do for his fans. "I am in superb condition and intend to keep that way," the young champ said. I would like nothing better than a crack at the Canadian Lightweight

Crown. I think I have proved in my victories over Jones, Robert, Speight and Thibault, that I am a very worthy contender."

Gardiner went on to credit his manager and trainer Johnny Cechetto for the progress he had made in the ring to that time. According to Gardiner, Cechetto spent his own money and invested his time at no cost to get Gardiner ready for the national lightweight crown. For Gardiner, Johnny Cechetto was the grandest guy in boxing. "He wasn't just a good boxing instructor. He was like a father to me. If I ever had any problems, I knew I could always go to him."

Writing in his boxing diary in 1961, Tyrone Gardiner stated some of his reasons for wanting to win the Canadian Championship. It wasn't all about himself.

"The fight game owes a lot to John for what he has done to keep it alive in Cape Breton. He said he hoped all his hard work would bring him a Canadian champion some day. He has tried with other fighters from time to time and he was always let down one way or another. I hope I can be the one to get a Canadian title for him and show him all the long hard fights he spent in the game were not in vain."[14]

Following his victories over Speight and Thibault, Gardiner soon became ranked the number one contender to take on Les Sprague for the Canadian Junior Welterweight Championship. A semi-final match was set up between Gardiner and Montrealer Fernand Simard, ranked number two, to decide who would get to box Sprague for the Canadian title. Gardiner was convinced he could defeat Sprague and Cechetto claimed his fighter was never in better shape. The Gardiner-Simard fight was promoted by Gussie MacLellan and held at the Northside Forum in North Sydney. The main event of the night was a fight between Blair Richardson and Vern LaMar.

The *Cape Breton Post* described the Gardiner-Simard fight as a "ding dong battle." The fight was refereed by Gordie MacDougall, a veteran of many ring battles himself. From the *Post* the next day:

"Gardiner and Simard put on a battle that was terrific from the opening bell and the fans where given reason to make with the applause pretty early as each battler came up with a lot of solid socking. They staged a good starting round and the bout never let up until the fifth was over and then it was announced the Montrealer was unable to come out. The third round was the thriller as Gardiner was facing his best opponent yet with Simard being bulldozer tough, and connecting on hard short chops. Gardiner had his opponent on the ropes twice in the fourth round but was unable to set him up for a finishing job. In the fifth round the Sydney River boy had the best of the going although he couldn't finish."[15]

Aubrey Keizer, writing in his Sportcycle column in the *Cape Breton Post* described the fight as Tyrone Gardiner's "greatest performance before Cape Breton boxing fans." Keizer said, "All five rounds were packed with action and on several occasions they fought toe-to-toe. The second round was one of the toughest rounds ever seen in a Cape Breton ring. For the fifteen minutes of the five rounds there wasn't a dull moment."

With Simard out of the way, Gardiner now had a clear path to a Canadian title shot. The only thing in his way was the indomitable Les Sprague of Amherst. When they arrived in Sydney in late April, 1963, to meet Gardiner for the third time, Tommy McCluskey, Sprague's trainer, described his boy as being in tip-top condition and ready for the fight of his life. Gardiner, who was usually rather soft spoken, made no bones about his "mounting dislike for the champion" in the local newspapers in the days coming up to the fight. "Sprague likes to overpower his opponent with his brawling tactics and is not beyond throwing a rabbit punch to meet his objective.... I have the advantage of two previous fights to draw my strategy and I can assure you that force will be meet with force."[16]

According to Russ Doyle in the *Cape Breton Post*, Gardiner proved the aggressor throughout the May 18 fight but Sprague "crouched, bobbed and weaved from side to side

Fig. 5.6. Tyrone Gardiner vs. Buddy Daye. Garndiner wins by TKO in fourth round. 1963. Photographer unknown. Courtesy Tyrone Gardiner.

Fig. 5.7. Standing: John Cechetto, Rudy Plichie. Seated (left to right): Johnny Devison, Glace Bay mayor John A. MacDonald and boxing chairman Andy MacDougall. 1960. Photographer unknown. Courtesy Rudy Plichie.

to avoid good shots intended for the head and body."[17] The only knockdown in the fight occurred in the tenth round when Sprague sent Gardiner to the mat with a looping right hook. Referee Bobby Beaton, a Port Hood native who officiated in more than 500 main events, 41 Canadian championships, a world championship and is credited with introducing the three-judge system to boxing, gave Gardiner until a count of eight to recover his stance and then the challenger retaliated immediately by opening a deep gash over Sprague's right eye. Sprague was able to weather Gardiner's onslaught and ended the fight bleeding profusely from above the eye while Gardiner was spouting blood from his nose. The twelve round bout, which Gardiner hoped and felt would finally give him a national crown, didn't end as he wished. Two of the three judges felt Sprague was the best fighter and voted as such. The champion Les Sprague retained his Canadian Junior Welterweight title with a split decision. Russ Doyle felt it was Sprague's "explosive left hook and crouching style" that helped him "pile up a lead in the early rounds when he out-pointed the challenger in their brief toe-to-toes skirmishes to come off the winner."

Though Gardiner failed in his third attempt to defeat Les Sprague, it did not deter him from his main goal, to become a Canadian champion, and after his third defeat to Les Sprague, Gardiner intensified his training by fighting a number of exhibition matches throughout Cape Breton. In 1963, he fought in Grand Anse, St. Peter's, Dominion, Port Hawkesbury, Whiteside, Ingonish and even the YMCA for children. Gardiner and manager Johnny Cechetto eventually got another chance at a Canadian title in October of 1963. The fight was for the vacant Canadian Lightweight Championship. The opponent was Marcel Gendron of Quebec City. Gendron, whose father Alfred Gendron was a top bantamweight in the 1930s, started boxing professionally at the age of fifteen. In 1960, Gendron won the Canadian Bantamweight title by knocking out Johnny Devison of Glace Bay in the seventh round of a fight waged in Sydney. Devison had obtained the title by beating Gendron in Montreal the previous year. Devison was a small, scrappy fighter who was in the navy. Like Eddie McKillop before him, Devison cleaned up most of his opponents in the Canadian Forces organized fights. He was the Atlantic Command Featherweight Champion in 1957. Devison's 1959 national title over Gendron was a forerunner of boxing victories in Cape Breton the likes of which had never been seen before.

As many fighters often do, either by virtue of age or deliberate diet and weight conditioning, Gendron moved up a weight class after the Devison loss. By the time he meet Tyrone Gardiner he was a junior lightweight and holder of the Canadian Featherweight title, which he won in a 1962 fight against Andre Millette. His record at the time was 23-5 with 16 knockouts.

Gardiner was such a respected athlete among the Cape Breton boxing fraternity and the community at large that he had no trouble getting help when he began to train for an important match, such as the upcoming fight against Gendron. The business community was always quick to help out the young champion when he needed training equipment or travel expenses. Art Pollett, the druggist, provided Gardiner with bandages and other medical supplies. Bill Stephens of J. W. Stephens Building Supplies of Sydney bought Gardiner his bathrobe, while Dave Epstein, a local merchant, supplied him with shoes and robes including a black silk one. Gardiner states, "I may not have been the best fighter going into the ring but I was the best dressed in the dressing room."[18]

Fig. 5.8. Sydney clothing merchant Dave Epstein and Tyrone Gardiner. Abbass Studios Collection, Beaton Institute, Cape Breton University, 21806.

From the boxing community, Gardiner credits Blair Joseph, Rocky MacDougall and Ronnie Sampson for helping him get in condition for the Marcel Gendron bout. In addition to his fellow boxing peers and his untiring manager Johnny Cechetto, one of the other members of the Cape Breton ring world at the time who knew of Gardiner's chances for success was cut man Rudy Plichie. According to Gardiner, Plichie never took "one cent" for all the hard work he did during the fighter's many ring battles. Plichie described Gardiner as the strongest lightweight he had ever worked with. As Plichie puts it, "He had remarkable recuperative power with correct body alignment, which was flexible to either attack or defend. That gave his punches a shock-like effect. There was no warning prior to delivery from any angle. He was a terrific body puncher with a lot of ring generalship." According to Plichie, when Gardiner's title was at stake he left the ring victorious. He was never in a dull fight, never ducked a challenge or contender for his title, and was always exciting to watch.[19]

The excitement around the 1963 fight for the Canadian Lightweight championship began to reach a fever pitch in Cape Breton in the fall. Not only was a local boy in it, but the fight was going to be fought in his hometown of Sydney, Nova Scotia. The old Sydney Forum, home to many bloodbaths on and off the ice, was the venue.

Thousands of fans were expected to attend. Everyone was interested in the fight and anyone who could get a ticket was going, with a couple of exceptions. Surprisingly, Tyrone Gardiner's father so disliked the sport he refused to go to any of his son's fights. His mother, always worried that he would get hurt, never went either. Gardiner says, "I knew they supported me, though, because they always threw a party for me at the house after I won a fight."[20]

In the weeks leading up to the title match against Marcel Gendron, Gardiner began to train at a furious pace. Johnny Cechetto and Gardiner had studied Gendron's technique and expected a lot a speed from the opponent.[21] To counter this speed, Gardner would try to corner him as much as possible. Gardiner trained day and night to the point many observers felt he was overworking himself and would burn out before the fight. Cechetto felt that since his boxer was feeling fine it was best to continue on the training regime they were using. Gardiner states that he didn't know anything about scientific boxing and lacked any kind of ring style. "I'd just plant myself in the ring and keep fighting till the round was over." He claims his advantages came from strength and endurance.

Two weeks before the match, Gardiner began to have second thoughts about himself in the ring. "What happens if I get knocked out after all the help that I was getting from everyone in and out of the ring," he said. "It would be very hard to live with if it should happen." Gardiner also feared that Gendron's handlers knew the Sydney boxer wasn't the most technical of fighters and they would use this against him. Ultimately it was thoughts like this that forced Gardiner to fight at his best.

Prior to the fight, Gendron, speaking via his manager, Frankie Belanger, who translated French into English for him, said to the press in Sydney, "I trained long and hard for this fight and if I don't leave here with the title it will only be because I met a superior opponent. Gardiner is a good fighter. I saw him against Fernand Simard in North Sydney last year. But I didn't come all this way to lose."[22]

On the night of October 26, 1963, the three-title holder from Ashby was as ready as he would ever be to take his first Canadian championship. The Sydney Forum was packed. Both fighters felt confident they had what it took to become champion. According to Russ Doyle in the *Cape Breton Post*, "The fighters paced themselves in the first two rounds before Gardiner took command early in the third. A barrage of rights and lefts to the body and a sharp left hook to the head dropped Gendron to one knee along the ropes for the first knockdown."[23] Gendron took a nine count, resumed fighting then went down a second time for a count of six. In the fourth round Gardiner delivered a long overhand right that sent his opponent to the deck. Gendron was able to rise, stumble off to a neutral corner only to be attacked again. Gardiner battered Gendron through the ropes and referee Bobby Beaton quickly ended the fight.

Russ Doyle described the fight as a "decisive technical knockout victory" in which Gardiner employed a "blistering two-fisted attack that sent Gendron to the canvas on four occasions." Tyrone Gardiner recalls how the fight went:

"Gendron was down in every round. This was a man who had never been off his feet in the ring, and he'd never been knocked out. It surprised me that he went down as easily as he did. I hit him hard in the first round, and I knew I had him right then. He never recovered from that first punch. Finally he went down again in the fourth round and didn't get up. I felt really good about winning, real good."[24]

Gendron remarked after the fight, "He's a good fighter. He proved it tonight. His punching was just too much for me." Gendron's trainer Frankie Belanger felt his fighter wasn't as sharp as usual but then remarked, "Gardiner didn't give him much of a chance." The victory over Marcel Gendron in Sydney not only gave Tyrone Gardiner the Canadian Lightweight Championship, it also gave him his fourth title, which in boxing circles is a hard earned distinction to come by. Gardiner also gave trainer Johnny Cechetto his first Canadian champion. Both men couldn't have been happier. The victory for fans was even sweeter because coupled with the 1959 Johnny Devison victory it was the second Canadian title held by a Cape Bretoner in recent years.

Fig. 5.9 Tyrone Gardiner in Venetian Gardens gym. 1960s. Photographer unknown. Courtesy Tyrone Gardiner.

Gardiner started the new year with a Canadian Championship title in one hand and a hard fought loss to Dick French of Providence, Rhode Island, in the other. Gardiner and French squared off in early January in Boston. French, the New England Welterweight Champion, dropped Gardiner four times in the fight before finishing the Sydney native in the first minute of the seventh round. In early 1964, John O'Rourke, a promoter from Long Island, New York, contacted Gardiner to arrange a fight between him and Dick DiVola, the New England Lightweight Champion. The fight was scheduled for February, but was called off because of an injury to DiVola. O'Rourke then booked Gardiner for an April fight against Johnny Bizarro in Erie, Pennsylvania. Unfortunately, Gardiner was disappointed again as that fight was also cancelled.

Gardiner's next fight was in June, 1964, when he took on Willie Williams in a ten-round, non-title fight at the Glace Bay Forum. Williams was from New Victoria but was fighting out of Boston at the time. Williams was just a youngster when he began working out with Johnny Nemis, Tommy "Gun" Spencer and the Hannigans. Williams started training with Spencer and eventually moved over to work with Johnny Nemis on Spencer's recommendation. "Johnny was a good trainer and he got a bunch of us to a good start. Blair, Gordie MacDougall and me, we all got going with him. Johnny was the key trainer back then," Williams said in a 2009 interview.[25] He eventually joined the Canadian army and racked up a number of titles while in the forces. Upon discharge he moved to Boston and began boxing out of the New Garden Gym.

In a 2009 interview in the *Cape Breton Post* with Greg MacNeil, Williams talked about his father and how he gave his children (five boys and four girls) boxing gloves in order to settle their differences. "Dad was a wonderful man and he'd send us to our beautiful backyard when we had kids had arguments," Williams recalls. "He said 'If you want to fight, get out there and put the gloves on'." Those backyard fights encouraged the young Williams to seek out the likes of Johnny Nemis and Johnny Cechetto as his early trainers. Williams was quickly lured away to the "big fight town of Boston" but eventually made it back to his native soil due to the shrewd promoting skills Gussie MacLellan.[26]

MacLellan arranged for the 1964 match between Williams and Gardiner realizing it would help draw an even bigger crowd than usual because it was between two local boys and was on the undercard of the match between Del Flanagan and the great middleweight, Blair Richardson. Williams was a sparring partner for Richardson at the time, who was also training in Boston. Williams today regards Richardson as a boxing legend and recalls being around him and other boxers such as Gordie MacDougall was a pleasure.[27] "I even used to spar with Blair though he was in a heavier class than me. We'd go at it for eight rounds sometimes and those guys from Boston would ask why we fought each other. I'd say because we Canucks got to stay together. Blair was my main man when we were in Boston and I'd love to come back home to fight sometimes on the same card with him," Williams said.[28]

The fact that he was returning to Cape Breton to fight Gardiner was an ironic twist of fate for Williams. "Knowing Tyrone Gardiner, we were at the same gym and then down the road we ended up fighting each other, it was just something you read about. You don't think it could happen to you," said Williams in 2009.[29] "You know even though we fought each other we became best friends," said Williams.[30]

Gardiner recalls that Williams was a fast fighter who could move from left to right and in and out extremely quickly, making him a hard target to hit. The fight went the distance with Williams winning by decision, despite the fact he had a severe cut over one eye. Williams credited his corner man, Charlie Pappas from Boston, with stopping the bleeding and allowing him to continue fighting to the end.

The *Cape Breton Highlander* reported that Gardiner, who was "well conditioned but far from sharp in his punching, was frustrated most of the way by the educated Williams jab which closed his left eye and kept him continually off balance.... Urged on by an excited hometown following, Williams seemed to pick up steam as Gardiner began to tire in the late going."[31] The unanimous victory against the reigning champion put Williams in the number one spot for a title match against Gardiner, said Canadian Boxing Federation chairman Dick Pearson, who was at ringside for the fight. In 2009 Gardiner still vividly remembers the fight. "He was an awfully hard target. When I fought him the first time he out boxed me."[32]

One of the requirements of holding a Canadian title at the time was that the champ had to defend his title at least once every six months provided the boxing commission could find a suitable challenger. The Williams rematch and title bout that fans were anxious for would have to wait, though, because a title match with Ferdinand "The Bull" Chretien of Toronto was next for Gardiner. Chretien got his nickname during his amateur days around the Palace Pier in Toronto. He came to town with a pro record of 19-2-2. In the previous year he had knocked out seven of his last eight opponents and won the other match by decision. Chretien was described in the local papers as a "rugged, crowd-pleasing opponent." This was to be a very important fight in Tyrone Gardiner's career because, after winning the Canadian title, he had lost his next two fights.

Gardiner recalls that "The Bull" arrived three days before the fight with his manager "Sully" Sullivan and two friends who had lots of money to toss around. They went to the gym every day looking to make bets that Chretien could easily stop the Ashby boy and local hero. Bobby Moore, a boxer from Sydney Mines who was living in Toronto, showed up at the gym asking around if anyone had ever seen Chretien fight. He told Gardiner the fight wasn't going to go very long because Chretien was going to stop him early on. To hear this from a boxer he had trained with for a number of years wasn't much help to the champion. Gardiner says that even the newspapers were putting their odds on the Toronto fighter.[33]

Thinking back on his career, Gardiner says that his title defense against "The Bull" Chretien was the toughest and best fight he fought. From the minute the fight started Gardiner knew he was in for the

Fig. 5.10. Gardiner defends (and wins) Canadian lightweight championship vs Ferdinand "The Bull" Chretien (left). Referee Bob Beaton. 1965. Photographer unknown. Courtesy Tyrone Gardiner.

The Bull & Tyrone & Bob Beaton

battle of his life. "He bulled across the ring and starting beating me from port to port. He rubbed me so hard on the ropes when I got back to the corner I was covered in rope burns," recalls Gardiner. "Every round we'd come out to the center of the ring, stood toe to toe and start punching. Neither one of us budged."[34]

Gardiner suffered a deep cut over his eye in the first round and credits cut man Rudy Plichie with keeping him in the fight. In round two the bleeding started up again and then some, thanks to a flurry of blows from The Bull, and Gardiner made it back to his stool with not one bloody eye but two. Rudy had all of thirty seconds to quell the flow of blood, which he miraculously was able to do. Gardiner remembers that in round three he thought he was losing the fight, even though his corner told him he was doing fine and to keep it up. The ring doctor had to come in after the third round to make sure both fighters could go on, as both men were now bleeding. The doctor gave his okay, repairs were made and soon round four was under way. The bloodbath continued. "It was the bloodiest fight of my life," recalls Gardiner. "I went down for the count of eight for the fourth straight round." Gardiner was fearful he would lose the fight but was able to finish the fourth round on his feet. Blood was everywhere.

The *Cape Breton Highlander* described Gardiner as a Toreador as he fought the Bull from Toronto, and stated that the bout "looked like a throwback to the bare knuckle days.[35] From the opening bell when they locked horns and rolled to the canvas in a wrestling hold, the two battlers went after each other with a vengeance that had old timers muttering about the days of "Terrible" Terry McGovern." The *Highlander* stated, "It was one of the wildest fights staged here in a long time.... Bleeding profusely from the second round on, Chretien set a hectic pace but found his bulling tactics nullified by Gardiner's superior strength at close quarters." In the fifth round Gardiner states he was lucky to hit The Bull with a hard straight right hand that cut his eyebrow wide open. The referee, Bobby Beaton, had no choice but to stop the fight and award it to Gardiner by way of a technical knock out. According to Gardiner, it was the worst beating he took in the ring in twelve years of professional boxing. Gardiner is convinced he would not have won the fight if it weren't for cut man Rudy Plichie and his repair jobs.

In the legacy of Cape Breton boxing, the eyebrow injuries that took their toll on Rockabye Ross and ultimately led to his downfall, actually worked to Tyrone Gardiner's advantage. "The Bull" Chretien had his eyebrow actually torn off in that final round by Gardiner. It had to be sewn back on at the hospital. While Chretien was taken to the hospital, Gardiner was in his dressing room, according to the *Cape Breton Highlander*, "wringing the blood and sweat out of his trunks."[36] Above it all, though, making the punishment and pain worthwhile, Gardiner had successfully defended his Canadian title.

Ferdinand "The Bull" Chretien returned to Toronto and eventually became a well-respected boxing referee. After that one bloody battle, he and Tyrone Gardiner became good friends and went on to keep in touch and exchange cards and letters for years. Chretien appeared in the 2004 Russell Crowe boxing film *Cinderella Man*, as a referee.

With the Canadian Championship still secure, the next obvious step for Gardiner was to fight for the British Empire Lightweight title. Rudy Plichie took on the task of arranging the fight but the British promoters wouldn't go for it. Without any chance of fighting for this crown, Gussie MacLellan arranged for Gardiner to take on Willie Williams again, this time in a title match. The fight would be a twelve-rounder, set to go on September 6, 1965, at the Glace Bay Miners Forum. Johnny Cechetto obtained fast sparring partners for Gardiner so the fighter could work on his speed. Gardiner also did a lot of fast handwork with Plichie. Plichie recalls that both fighters were always the type to keep in top condition. The night of the fight, Gardiner felt he was in excellent shape and had a firm hold on his title.[37] However, Gardiner also felt some apprehension about the rematch and was worried that if Williams took him the entire twelve rounds then Williams would come out the victor.[38]

Opening the fight with a barrage of body blows, fans felt that Gardiner was going for the quick knockout.[39] In the second, Williams took a solid right hook to the chin that appeared to have hurt him. In the third round, Gardiner was punishing Williams with body shots, hard punches to the stomach and ribs, all the while throwing out big rights in search of Williams's chin again. By the fourth round, Gardiner had put Williams down twice. Williams managed to hold on until the bell without falling again, which would have ended the fight as the Three-Knockdown Rule was in effect. Williams seemed to come alive in the fifth, when suddenly his jab seemed to be working, not just keeping the champ at bay but doing some damage, too. At times, those at ringside felt Gardiner might have punched himself out, this coupled with the fact that Williams looked even stronger in the sixth. But also in the sixth Gardiner began to pace himself better, and seemed to be regaining control of the fight from the game Williams. In the seventh, Gardiner bounded from his corner and rocked Williams with a devastating right to his chin. It was the punch Gardiner had been looking for all night and it was

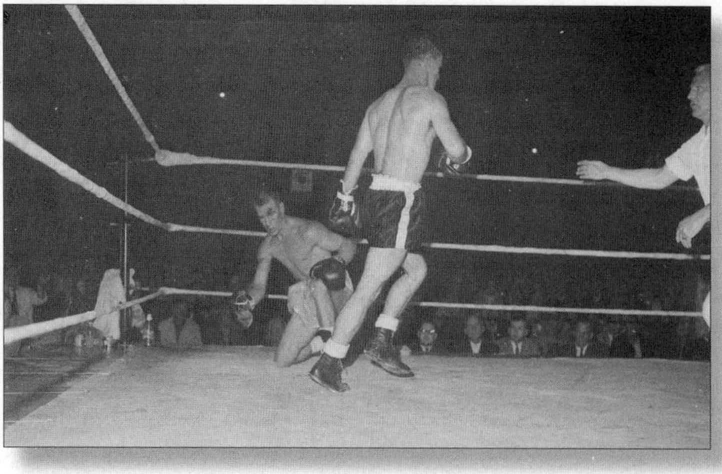

Fig. 5.11. Tyrone Gardiner vs. Willie Williams (down) for Canadian lightweight championship. Sept. 6, 1965. Abbass Studios Collection, Beaton Institute, Cape Breton University, B-3966b.

lights out for the challenger. For the second time, Tyrone Gardiner had defended his Canadian Lightweight crown. And with another noble nod to the respect and camaraderie that personified the fight game in those days, Williams, like Chretien, became good friends with his opponent Gardiner, and the two stayed in touch long after they'd retired from boxing.

Looking back on the fight, Gardiner had this to say in 2009: "The second fight was different than the first. It was all heavy punching. It slowed him down. He was a different fighter when he wasn't up on his toes and bouncing around. He was sharp. He could move left and right, in and out."[40]

Fig. 5.12. Victorious, Gardiner celebrates victory over Williams with jubilant fans and friends. 1965. Abbass Studios Collection, Beaton Institute, Cape Breton University, B-3966e.

Williams recalls the fight much the same. "We fought and we shook hands afterward. We boxed toe-to-toe and then would go over and hug each other at the end. People couldn't figure out what was going on."[41]

Right after the Williams victory, Gussie MacLellan announced that negotiations were underway for a fight between Gardiner and Bunny Grant of Jamaica, the British Empire title holder. This would have been the pinnacle of Tyrone Gardiner's boxing career, but unfortunately it was not to be. Due to circumstances beyond the Cape Breton champion's control, the details were never worked out and the fight never came off. For months afterwards, Rudy Plichie continued with the attempt to get Gardiner a shot at the British Empire title, though it was never in the cards.

Fight fans had hoped that Gardiner and Williams would fight a rubber match but that bout never got arranged either. Both fighters to this day regret never having a chance to fight the rubber match. Williams returned to the Massachueusetts area and spent many years after boxing as a court officer. Due to other commitments, Gardiner decided to stop boxing on a winning note. In September, 1966, he made it official. He was leaving boxing on top, holding the titles to the Nova Scotia, Maritime, Eastern Canadian and Canadian Lightweight championships. He finished his career with a record of 73-9-4 and was never knocked out.

After hanging up the gloves for good, Gardiner worked as a guard at the county correctional center for twenty-three years, ran a successful gas station, got involved with raising horses, ran an antique business and for a time was a concert promoter. He was involved with others in bringing the legendary

Fig. 5.13. As a promoter, Tyrone Gardiner brought acts like Johnny Cash and June Carter Cash to Sydney. Courtesy Tyrone Gardiner.

Johnny Ty June

singer Johnny Cash to Cape Breton on two different occasions. Tyrone and his wife Flora [MacKeigan] have one son, Jamie who works in Australia and spends his free time equestrian horse riding. For a while he trained with the famous Canadian Olympian Ian Miller. Today Gardiner and his wife reside in Mira with their dog and horses.

Though he stopped boxing, Tyrone Gardiner never actually left the ring and has been involved with promoting the sport in Cape Breton for decades. Often he and his pal Rudy Plichie can be seen putting up posters for upcoming amateur fights being held in the local area. Gardiner says that boxing, as well as other sports, gives you a different perspective on life. "It helps you gain self-confidence when you know you're good at something. You don't need to prove yourself to anyone."[42] Reflecting on his years as a jail guard Gardiner says he'd see parents coming in to bail out their troubled children. "If only they'd spent the bail money ahead of time on getting the kids into sports or something, maybe it would have kept them out of trouble."[43] In 2003, Gardiner was inducted in the World Boxing Hall of Fame. An honor befitting a great Cape Breton athlete and role model who fought with dignity and finished in style.

Fig. 5.14. Opposite: Poster promoting Tyrone Gardiner's induction into the Boxing Hall of Fame. 1987. Courtesy Rudy Plichie.

Canadian Champion
Tyrone Gardiner

BOXING NEWS

CLASS OF 1987

Distinction earned. Recognition deserved.

CANADIAN BOXING HALL OF FAME

TYRONE GARDINER
SYDNEY RIVER
Canadian Lighweight Champion

Nova Scotia
Boxing Record: Amateur and Professional
63 wins, 4 losses.
3 draws
Height: 5 ft. 6 1/2 in.
Weight: 135 lbs.
RING STYLE:
Box and Weaver, very explosive. Well disciplined athlete - campaigned with considerable success for 12 yrs.
Retired undefeated light weight champion of Canada.

Highlights of Career:
1960 - Won Cape Breton - Nova Scotia Title's.
1961 - Won Maritime Light Weight Title.
1961 - Won Eastern Canadian Light Weight Title.
1963 - Won Canadian Light Weight Title.
Tyrone Gardiner achieved extraordinary distinction in the sport of Boxing. His accomplishments are too numerous to write about.
It is with pride the following are inducted into the Hall of Fame of the Nova Scotia Sport Heritage Centre.

TYRONE GARDINER
SYDNEY RIVER
Canadian Lighweight Champion

to the
Nova Scotia Sports Heritage Centre

RETIRED
UNDEFEATED
CANADIAN
LIGHTWEIGHT
CHAMPION
OF CANADA
IN 1966
WITH ALL FOUR TITLES

retired undefeated
Canadian Lightweight Champion
1963-66
John Cechetto, manager

THE VERY BEST TO ALL MEMBERS OF THE CANADIAN BOXING HALL OF FAME

ROUND SIX:
BLAIR RICHARDSON, BOXER, TEACHER, PREACHER

In many ways, Cape Breton's love affair with boxing during the 1950s and 1960s grew out of Bucky Sampson's Steelworkers Hall gym on Prince Street in Sydney. Around the same time that future Canadian Lightweight Champion Tyrone Gardiner was water boy at Sampson's gym, there was a blond, good looking and always smiling kid by the name of Blair Richardson who'd also taken an interest in the sport of boxing. Richardson, the son of Leland and Christina Richardson,

Fig. 6.1. Blair Richardson. *Cape Breton Post*, 1962. Courtesy Karl Marsh.

who hailed from South Bar, a tiny community on the outskirts of Whitney Pier, went on to be regarded by those in the Cape Breton boxing community as one of the finest athletes to ever set foot in the ring. A gentleman to all who knew him, Richardson was, on the surface, something of a contradiction. A shy, reserved and soft-spoken man who many would describe as one of the friendliest and most polite people they had ever met; yet, he also happened to possess in his right fist a savage force that could knock down walls. It was a profound punching power that, despite Richardson's true disposition of erudition and non-violence, would

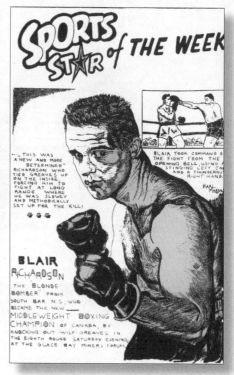

wreak physical devastation on dozens of opponents in the ring. One of the finest middleweights in Canadian boxing history and a serious contender for a world crown, the story of Cape Bretoner Blair Richardson is one of dedication, hard work and triumph; but it's also a tale of misfortune and tragedy. To this day, the young fighter's untimely demise endures as one of the most heart-wrenching tragedies in Canadian sports history.

Even during those early days at Sampson's gym, Richardson stood out as a young boxer with promise, a dazzling prospect whose natural gifts and work ethic did not escape the all-seeing eye of veteran ring master Johnny Nemis. In the early stages of Richardson's career, Nemis acted as both manager and trainer for the future champion. The veteran South Bar boxer Gordie MacDougall was a regular at Sampson's gym in the days when the young Richardson first appeared on the scene, and in an interview in *Cape Breton Works* recalled his first encounters with the boxing prodigy.

Blair Richardson

"Blair Richardson was a terrific kid. He boxed when he was around 12 years old in a Golden Gloves. He was also a very shy kid, and that's the only time he fought. Then he started coming to the gym with me, carrying my bags. Then he'd come in the gym when I worked out in the afternoon to spar with me. He was always shy, especially in front of a crowd. Then I got him coming at night, and he kept coming. He trained with me for about five years, until he was about 17 or 18."[1]

Leland Richardson remembers his son's dedication to boxing from an early time. "He lived to train. Every day he'd do roadwork or go to the gym. All the time it was gym, gym, gym, skipping, the punching bag out in the garage, running to the lake and back."[2]

Richardson's pro career began on Dominion Day, 1956, when he knocked out a local fighter named Tiger Dorrington in the fourth round.[3] This would be the first of thirty-six knockouts

Fig. 6.2.
Blair Richardson.
Photographer unknown.
Courtesy Tyrone Gardiner.

that Richardson would record in his career. He fought two more times in 1956, knocking out both Jimmy Desmond and Jim Stewart, respectively. Richardson fought four times in 1957, winning two bouts by knockout, fighting to a draw with George Bonovich, and losing to New Glasgow fighter Al MacLean. What's remarkable about this first stage of Richardson's career is the fact that he was born in 1941, which means that by the time he had this first string of professional bouts under his belt he was all of 16 years old.

In 1958, Richardson fought four more times, winning each match by knockout. His four opponents lasted a cumulative total of just eight rounds. Also during that watershed year, *Ring Magazine*, the foremost boxing publication in North America, chose the power-punching Cape Bretoner as the best prospect in the world in the middleweight division. *Ring* founding editor Nat Fleischer figured Richardson to be the eighth contender in line for Dick Tiger's world middleweight crown.[4] All this, and Blair Richardson had yet to turn eighteen.

Stan McPhail[5] of Sydney, a keen and knowledgeable observer of the local fight game, remembers the early days of Blair Richardson's career. "Blair and I would often walk to the gym together and sometimes leave together and wait for the bus. There was this one night Johnny Nemis called Blair back into the gym as we were leaving. I waited for him outside. When Blair came back outside he asked me, 'Do you know why he called me back inside?' I said no. Blair said, 'He asked me if I wanted to be Canadian champ. What do you think of that Stan?' I said go for it, buddy. If Johnny thinks you can do it, you can do it." McPhail and others who were around the fight scene in Sydney in the 1950s credit Johnny Nemis with the ability to recognize a winner at an early age. "If you got serious, then Johnny could make you a champ," said McPhail. Evidently, Blair Richardson decided it was time to get serious.

Stan McPhail's younger brother Walter remembers that Richardson would always be hanging around their place in South Bar either training or quoting bible verses with the McPhail's father Collie. "He was into religion and boxing at the same time," said Walter. "I remember he

Fig. 6.3.
Dempsey McPhail.
Courtesy Stan McPhail.

asked me once when he was getting started if he could take my older brother Dempsey in a fight."[6] Dempsey McPhail was quite the boxer in his own right. He left the McPhail clan at a young age and worked as a stevedore in New York for years, boxing along the way and crossing paths with many American fighters including the notorious Jake LaMotta. "Demps used to box with dad and there'd be bloodbaths at home," said McPhail. At the time, the McPhails didn't realize their friend and neighbor Blair Richardson would eventually end up in the States just like their older brother did.

In 1959, Richardson continued his winning ways with an astonishing ten straight knockouts, and in June of that year took the Maritime middleweight crown in convincing fashion, knocking out Nick Kovac in the third round. By October, Richardson held the Eastern Canadian title as well, having put Montreal native Yvon Turenne to the floor in six. Richardson finished the year with an eighth-round knockout in Halifax over the always dangerous Cliff "Bobo" Fiddler of Prince Albert, Saskatchewan. However, unfortunately for Richardson, he cracked a bone in a finger of his right hand that would sideline him for several months.[7] This would be the first of many problems with his hands and fingers that Richardson would have to endure. Why? As described by the online boxing encyclopedia, BoxRec, Richardson was a hard-punching middleweight "who hit too hard for his own good. The bones of his fists were unable to withstand his tremendous punching power, causing him to suffer several bone fractures throughout his career."[8] Meanwhile *Boxing Illustrated* magazine called Richardson's hands brittle and Halifax fight official Murray Sleep said they were, "the smallest pair of hands for a middleweight that I ever saw in my life."[9]

Gordie MacDougall was one of Richardson's sparring partners during the days when he was first lacing gloves onto those brittle hands and Stan McPhail remembers watching Richardson and MacDougall go at it one night as Richardson prepared for an upcoming fight. "When Blair started fighting he was one of the most awkward fellows on his feet," says McPhail.

"He had terrible feet. He could never dance back. He'd trip over his feet. Gordie was a natural, though. He could dance like Muhammad Ali. This night, Gordie was coming at Blair and he had him on the

Fig. 6.4.
Blair Richardson.
Courtesy Tyrone Gardiner.

ropes. Gordie would never back up. The punches were coming from everywhere. I was timekeeper that night and there was about a minute to go in the round. I looked at Johnny (Nemis) and gestured if I should ring the bell. Johnny shook his head no. Blair finally got through the round and survived." McPhail recalls that from that night on he began to closely watch Richardson and MacDougall as they trained. Soon enough, Richardson's issues with footwork improved. "All of a sudden, Blair wasn't tripping over his feet. He was standing the ground calling for Gordie to come after him. After a while it was Gordie who was backing up. Blair did that (took so much punishment) because he was so determined to learn. Blair had to work hard."

Fig. 6.5. Blair Richardson in Boston. Clipping courtesy Whitney Pier Historical Society.

Richardson works out sometimes with Boston Bruins and talks with goalie Ed Johnston in dressing room.

In 1960, Richardson moved to Boston to continue training under the guidance of Johnny Buckley. Buckley's gym was a murky, sweat-soured second floor space in an old building on Friend Street, as described by news writer Joe Smith.[10] According to Robert Ashe, Buckley was a bitter, crude and opinionated man in his 70s when Richardson first met him. Nonetheless, few people knew the game of boxing as well as Buckley.[11]

Richardson explained the reason for his move to the States in a phone conversation with his original trainer, Johnny Nemis. "I'm happy here because I have good sparring mates. It was not fair at home, to my sparring partners or myself. They were not encouraged, and it wasn't helping me. Up here I have good sparring mates. I'm learning and gaining experience."[12] That says a lot about Blair Richardson. Even his sparring partners liked and respected him so much that, when the opportunity presented itself, they couldn't bring themselves to seriously hurt him. Richardson himself must have sensed this, and so sought to remedy the situation by going to a place where he would not be surrounded by friends.

Sydney boxer Allie Steele recalls that Richardson's move to the States was a smart one. "Blair had a good head," says Steele. "He was very smart. He would promote pretty well all his later fights. Gussie MacLellan was involved but it was Blair that gave it the terms. He was the card. He was the draw. He said who he fought, when he fought and for how much."[13]

Richardson fought two bouts in early 1960 in Boston, winning both. He returned to Cape Breton in April to take on Al Rose of Massachusetts in a fight at the Glace Bay Miners Forum arranged by Gussie MacLellan. More than 3,000 fans showed up to watch the returning hero take on the brawling New Englander.

In the opening round, Rose rocked Richardson with a right to the jaw, and Richardson had to take a standing eight count before the fight was allowed to continue. Wisely, he stayed clear of Rose for the rest of the round. Richardson was able to shake off the first round and rebound in the second and Rose felt for the first time the punishing sting of a Richardson right. Rose very nearly went down but managed to hold on and remain in the match. But Richardson rocked him again in the fifth and, mid way through the sixth, Richardson put Rose down for good. However, as Richardson stood in a neutral corner waiting for Rose to be counted out, the South Bar fighter also appeared to be in poor condition. He was holding his jaw with both hands and spitting large amounts of blood. After clearing the ring, Richardson was examined by Art Ormiston, boxing commission doctor, and then rushed to Sydney City Hospital.[14]

For those at ringside that night, the first round punch that Richardson took on the jaw seemed like just another clean, hard blow. But Richardson's manager Johnny Nemis and his trainer Leo Pratt both knew it was more than that. Unbeknownst to Rose, he had actually broken Richardson's jaw with that first punch. Pratt immediately wanted to stop the fight, but Richardson was adamant that the fight continue. Afterward, Richardson was heard to say, "I was in the ring and they could count me out or carry me out. A lot of people paid to see a fight, and I didn't want to see them disappointed." Richardson figured his jaw got broken because his mouth had been slightly open when Rose had hit him. The day after the fight a surgeon wired Richardson's jaw back together and the blond slugger from South Bar sucked his meals through a straw for the next two months.[15]

Al Rose had fought eighteen bouts prior to his meeting with Richardson and had won all but one. He was tough. The real deal. "I was told he was a solid socker," said Rose of Richardson following the fight. "But I had no idea he was such a terrific hitter. I didn't fully recover from that blow in the second round, and I couldn't get going right after that."

Though hockey—and in some ways soccer and basketball—have replaced boxing as the sport of the masses in Cape Breton today, these sports do not carry the burning desire for a champion that boxing did in its heyday. Certainly, Cape Bretoners will get behind one of their own that makes it all the way to the National Hockey League, but for a boxer that had the potential to go all the way, well, Cape Breton fight fans would follow that man anywhere. Part of this, of course, is the individuality of boxing itself. When you're a boxer, there are no teammates with you in the ring; there's no one in there to make you look good; and there is no one in there to help you. You are on your own. Cape Breton fight fans—indeed, fight fans the world over—clearly relate to this ancient test of the individual. It is not hard to imagine, after all, that it is *you* in that ring, and we can't help but wonder how we ourselves would fare under such conditions. Indeed, the "fight or flee" impulse that is hardwired into all of us is not an option. In the ring, there is nowhere to run; the only option is to fight, and that touches deep inside the human condition. It also helps to explain the powerful psychological pull that boxing has on the human heart and mind. It's a testament to the enduring popularity of the sport in practically every country in the world.

Add to this fact the elements of time and place. Small town 1950s North America. Despite the occasional "villain," boxers of this era were uniformly gentlemen. They didn't drink, they didn't smoke (how could they and sustain the punishing physical pace?) and they always exhibited the utmost respect for their opponents. To use the old saying, this was "old school" boxing, the sort that is simply not seen in the glitz and glamour of today's fight game. And Blair Richardson embodied this old school ethos perhaps more than any other boxer that Cape Breton has produced. He epitomized the gentleman fighter. Shy and reserved outside the ring, and above all, non-violent; but within the ring, a feared gladiator with the courage to take on all comers. Blair Richardson's character came to the fore in a letter of thanks he wrote to sportswriter Earle Pemberton in August, 1960, after that grueling match with Al Rose, a match in which he not only sustained a broken jaw, but also re-injured his right hand. Richardson wrote:

"Just a line to thank you for the very kind words you said about me on television last week. I only hope I can live up to that and at least be a credit to boxing. I enjoyed the program very much and I thought you were good on TV. You certainly know your boxing. That is another reason I appreciated what you said, because I, as well as others, respect your opinion on boxers and boxing."[16]

Veteran Halifax broadcaster Pat Connolly, who described Richardson as a charming individual who always ignited the public's imagination says in *Halifax Champion*, "We counted on him always to say something intelligent and he brought another dimension to the game—that of thoughtful expression."[17]

Richardson had plenty of time for thoughtful expression over the next five months as he recovered from the injuries that Rose inflicted on him. When he was cleared to fight again, his opponent was Ted "Roosevelt" Myrick and the fight was held before a wild crowd of 5,000 at the Halifax Forum. Throughout the first two rounds of the non-title bout, Richardson peppered Myrick with left jabs. In the third round, he staggered Myrick with several hard blows to the jaw and then cut him with a vicious right uppercut midway through the fourth before finishing him off with a fight-ending right to the jaw.[18] A month after the Myrick fight, Richardson was back in Glace Bay facing "the Baltimore Cutie" Johnny Cunningham. Cunningham had fought some of the best lightweights and welterweights in the world at that time, including three matches against Carmen Basilio, *Ring Magazine's* Fighter of the Year for 1957. Richardson started out slow and missed a chance to stop Cunningham in the fifth. The fight ended up going the distance with Richardson the victor by decision.[19]

On the first of November, 1960, Richardson defended his Eastern Canadian Middleweight crown against Yvon Turenne of Montreal. In front of 5,000 fans at the Halifax Forum, Richardson retained his title by putting Turenne to the mat in the seventh round. A few weeks later Richardson was back in Sydney reading in the *Cape Breton Post* comments made by his next opponent, Gene Hamilton of Brooklyn, New York. Hamilton is quoted as saying, "I know Richardson is a solid puncher, as shown by his record, but he's going to have trouble hitting me." No one could have been more wrong about Blair Richardson.

Richardson's onslaught got underway in the third round with a hard right that stunned the trash-talking New Yorker. He continued the barrage into the fourth and fifth rounds before finally knocking Hamilton down in the sixth. At the end of the eighth, Hamilton was bloodied and barely hanging on. Ever the gentleman, Richardson coasted through the ninth round, choosing to not inflict more punishment on Hamilton and allowing the New Yorker to give up on bended knee in the tenth. Referee Pordena Smith ruled it a technical knockout. Hamilton echoed his earlier comments about Richardson's punching ability but added, in somewhat more somber tones, "I knew Richardson could hit ... but never figured that hard."

Though Richardson handily took care of Hamilton, he injured his right hand again, which sidelined him for another five months. Compared to the long breaks in between boxing matches today, which are there to allow time for fighters to heal, it seems the only way to get time to recover from a fight in Richardson's era was to get injured to the point of breaking something.

Richardson didn't fight again till May, 1961, when he defeated Bobby Barnes of Pennsylvania in a lackluster ten-round affair at the Halifax Forum.

Johnny Nemis was in his corner for the fight. "Barnes was a cutie. He fought sideways and made it tough for Blair to get a good shot. Blair didn't favour the right hand, though. It was completely mended and we were ready," explained Nemis. Vernon Gilbert of the *Cape Breton Post* wrote that the only knockdown occurred in the sixth round when Richardson belted Barnes with a right cross that landed him in the neutral corner for a nine count. Barnes came on strong in the later rounds but to no avail. Gilbert stated Richardson appeared sluggish most of way and was jeered by fans because of his seemingly tepid performance.[20]

When in Halifax, Richardson often trained at the Creighton Street Gym. Charles Saunders, in his book *Sweat and Soul,* said that the gym, run by the Paris Brothers, was a wooden one-floor magnet for aspiring black Nova Scotian boxers in the 1950s, and that the Paris brothers "never drew the color line at their facility."[21] Though described in *Halifax Champion* as a single-storey structure down a dark alley between houses that had a speed bag, a punching bag, some skipping ropes, an occasional ring set up, and a bad smell, Keith and Percy Paris's ramshackle gym saw many great Halifax boxers come through its door to train.[22] These included Buddy Daye, Lennie Sparks and future Canadian Middleweight Champion David Downey. Richardson often trained there amongst the mainly black boxers from the local area. When Keith Paris would fight in Sydney he'd stay with Richardson's family. "I'd go there and Blair'd say, 'take my room' and 'look after my friend'. He treated me just like part of the family." Before Richardson's time, Joe Pyle of New Waterford, an African Canadian, was also a regular at the Creighton Street Gym, where fighters could train and spar before going to the house next door for a shower. The fighting fisherman Yvon Durelle was also known to occasionally drop into the Halifax gym.

Richardson fought again in Halifax at the end of the month. His opponent was Eskil "Swede" Emerson, who had eighteen wins and one draw in his twenty-four professional fights. He had, however, fought seventy-one amateur bouts in Sweden. After a slow first round, Richardson hit Emerson with a stiff right early in the second that sent him to a neutral corner. A straight left and a follow-up right cross dropped Emerson to the mat. The "Swede" got up only to be knocked down again. As he staggered to his feet, referee Jack Delaney decided he'd had enough and awarded Richardson a technical knockout.[23]

Richardson's dull performance from the month before was vindicated in this fight with Emerson. With the victory, Richardson had won a total of twenty-four fights in a row, of which all but two were knockouts. His performance was considered outstanding and all bets were on him to become the next middleweight champion of Canada. Every great champion can suffer a set-back, though, and Blair Richardson's set-back occurred on August 29, 1961.

Richardson was paired up against Burke Emery, a Quebec boxer who was Light Heavyweight Champion of Canada. The fight was a ten-round non-title bout held before 6,200 fans at the Halifax Forum. The fight was less than dramatic and all the officials had Richardson ahead on points going into the ninth round. Things changed in the ninth, though, when Emery released an unexpected flurry of well-placed punches. The sportswriter Ace Foley described the fight afterwards in the *Cape Breton Post*.

"Emery exploded unexpected dynamite in Richardson's own corner to knock the Eastern Canadian Middleweight champ down for the full count. The *coup-de-grat* came at a time when it looked like Richardson may take control. The ending came with dramatic suddenness. Richardson was opening Emery with a jarring left to the face when the Sherbrooke, Quebec fighter backed the Cape Bretoner into his own corner, crashed a left to the jaw followed by a blistering right to the same spot, threw in another left, and stepped back as Richardson crumpled to the deck while a doleful decimal was tolled over him. Referee Jack Delaney said the three finishing punches were 'squarely on the button'."[24]

In Richardson's own words, "The first thing I knew was that somebody told me I had lost the fight. There were no scars. In the first round I broke my left hand. I'm not making excuses. Maybe I became careless; maybe I figured Emery had punched himself out when the ninth came up."[25] Up until the knockout punch in the ninth, Emery had little chance to win, but in boxing, things can change in an instant.

Richardson returned to train in Boston after the Emery fight but was so remorseful about losing his first fight in twenty-five matches that he wrote to Earle Pemberton a couple of weeks later. The depth of feeling Richardson had for his fans, as well as his love of boxing, is summed up best in these few sentences that appeared in the November, 1961, issue of *Punching with Pemberton*.

Dear Mr. Pemberton,

I feel honoured that you did an article on me in your sports bulletin. I really enjoyed the story. That puts me along with the great old-timers, which you have been running in your paper. In the fighting department though I have a long way to go to equal them. Reading your article brought tears to my eyes because I had lost to Emery in Halifax and I know I disappointed many people including you. But Earle I tried my very best and it just wasn't enough. Maybe some day I'll be able to reverse that defeat. God willing. Thanking you for all the wonderful things you have done for me and if I'm not a credit to boxing one thing for sure you are, so keep up the good work. Your friend, Blair Richardson.[26]

If there was need to prove a boxer had heart, those words are proof beyond a doubt. Richardson's humble apology to his legions of fans in Cape Breton and throughout the Maritimes indicates the true essence of the young man and the future vocation he would take. But the loss to Emery did not dampen his spirits for long. In late October, Richardson was back in Halifax paired up against a tough light-heavyweight from New York by the name of Floyd McCoy.

By the second round of the October 30 fight, Floyd McCoy knew he was up against someone who could throw a powerful punch. McCoy took a shot in the second round that required a count of five for him to recover. By the time the bell sounded to end the round it appeared that McCoy had recovered because at the start of the next round he came out swinging. Richardson had to dodge McCoy's right a number of times. McCoy was clearly targeting Richardson's jaw, hopeful that since it had been broken before by Al Rose it might prove to be Richardson's Achilles heel. Richardson resorted to a defensive stance to ward off McCoy's attack, blocking a barrage of punches with his gloves and elbows before he was able to deliver a hard right to McCoy's own jaw. McCoy dropped to the canvas but was able to slowly get himself back up. The effort was in vain, though. Before any further punches were thrown, McCoy fell into the ropes and the referee wisely stopped the fight. The *Cape Breton Post* called the punch that floored McCoy a, "bone jarring right to the head." In all of three rounds, Blair Richardson had signaled to one and all that he was back in form.[27]

With the McCoy victory behind him, Richardson was anxious to avenge the loss he suffered at the hands of Burke Emery a couple of months before. A rematch between the two was set for November in Halifax. In preparation for the match, Richardson was training with Al Lacey of Boston. When fight night arrived, nearly 6,000 fans showed up to see if the Cape Bretoner could get even with Emery. As usual, busloads of Cape Bretoners arrived in Halifax to cheer on their local hero. By all accounts, the bout was a cautious affair for both fighters—until the last three rounds. "The best exchanges were on the ropes, when first Richardson would swing to the body and then to the head and then Emery would take over with a similar attack," wrote Ace Foley in the *Halifax Chronicle Herald*.[28] The fight went the distance with Richardson beating the Light Heavyweight Champion of Canada by a decision, although Emery's belt was safe because the fight had been a non-title match.

After the fight, Richardson said, "I won on my showing in the last two or three rounds. He hit me a couple of good punches but never hurt me. In the second round I sprained my right wrist and fought from then on practically one-handed. I tried to use the right several times, but the sharp pain ruled that out and I was not effective offensively from then on."[29]

Burned Greaves' Boxing Gloves When He Was Five

Wilfie Greaves was only five years old when his mother burned his boxing gloves. At the time, Wilf was raising lumps on children from neighboring farms in the Entwistle area, 60 miles west of Edmonton. Mrs. Max Greaves says her son's career as a boxer was fated. Wilf, the Canadian middleweight champion, has had some pretty important bouts in the U. S. and his home town, Edmonton.

"The minister who baptized Wolf said he would be a boxer," Mrs. Greaves said. She pronounces his name "Wolf", almost a nickname among his Edmonton friends. "Wilf never fought much at school," explains a former classmate. "After a couple of scrapes, nobody would fight with him."

Clean-Cut

Greaves is a handsome 27-year-old, with clean-cut features unmarred by ring scars. An average student, he took grade 12 and stayed away from schoolyard brawls. His career began when boxing instructor Bob Ford of Edmonton spotted him wrestling. Wilf trained hard, learning fast, and climaxed his amateur career by winning a British Empire Games title at Vancouver in 1954. The next year he turned pro.

When Wilf was managed by Jake Mintz he made Pittsburg his home and boxed throughout U. S. fight centres, fighting topnotchers such as Gene Fulmer, Ralph (Tiger) Jones, Al Andrews, Italo Scortichini, "Spider" Webb and Joey Giardello, before he had 20 pro matches. Some observers claimed he was being brought along too fast, but he improved steadily and on April 26, 1958, at Windsor, Ontario, he knocked out

WILFIE GREAVES
Canadian Middleweight Champion and former British Empire title holder. Born Dec. 7, 1935 at Edmonton, Alta. Height 5' 8½".

Cobey McCluskey in four rounds to win the vacant Canadian middleweight title.

Now With Larry Smith

When Mintz died, Wilf changed managers several times before signing up with C. W. (Larry) Smith, wealthy Detroit industrialist. Wilf, who maintains a Canadian residence in Windsor, fights out of Detroit

How does he like the game?

"I was always stubborn—a poor loser. Through boxing, I felt, I could let off steam and make it legal — legalized murder. Of course, you make a lot of friends. Some of the nicest guys I have known are in the boxing business. Then there are contacts . . . you make a lot of contacts while you are active; then when you retire you take advantage of them."

Wilf keeps his 155-pound body in splendid condition. He neither smokes nor drinks. Protein-high meals and two miles of roadwork each morning keep him in trim. Except for a nose slightly flattened by a butt, his face is unmarked.

(continued on page 4)

---

99 seconds in the first round. This was a six-rounder on the card headlined by heavyweights Willie Besmanoff and New Englander Tom McNeely, in Boston.

Blair is being handled in his Boston bouts by veteran trainer-manager Johnny Buckley.

On March 15, in a long-distance call to his manager Johnny Nemis Blair made the following statement: "I'm happy here because I have good sparring mates. It was not fair at home, to myself or my sparring partners. They were not encouraged, and it wasn't helping me. Up here I have good sparring mates. I'm learning and gaining experience."

In April, 1960, one of the greatest champions of all time, Mickey Walker, visited young Blair at Richardson's training camp in Boston. The one-time holder of world welter and middleweight crowns, Mickey gave young Blair some kind words of advice, and
(continued on page 2)

Five $10 Draws

№ 653

PUNCHING WITH PEMBERTON

VOL. 2, No. 4   AUGUST 1962   PRICE 25c

BLAIR RICHARDSON
A Review of His Boxing Career
By J. EARLE PEMBERTON

"We know how rough the road will be,
How heavy here the load will be;
We know about the barricades
that wait along the track;
But we have set our soul ahead
Upon a certain goal ahead,
And nothing left from hell to sky
shall ever turn us back."

* * * * *

Blair Richardson embarked on his boxing career in July 1956. He engaged in three bouts that year, all ending in knockouts.

In 1957 Richardson suffered his only loss when he dropped a close six-round decision to Al MacLean of New Glasgow, N. S. The following month one George Bonovich managed to get a six-round draw with Richardson but if Bonavich had chosen to fight instead of run, it certainly would have been a different story.

In 1958 Blair disposed of New Waterford's Russ Micholsky in less than one round, knocked out K. O. O'Malley in two rounds, got rid of Kenny Stokes in two, and stopped Alf Grant in three.

Busy Year

The year 1959 was a busy one for Blair. Starting January 14, he put Joe Scott away in three, kayoed rough, tough Tiger Steel in eight, and hung the K.O. sign on Nick Kovac in three to cop the Maritime middleweight title. He knocked out Wally Wilson in two, Al Duarte in five, Gaston Roy in eight; forced tough Yvon Turenne to quit in six to win the Eastern Canada middleweight crown; flattened Willie Troy in four, and with some of the stiffest punching ever displayed in Halifax Forum, Blair hung a TKO on tough Bobo Fiddler of Prince Albert, Saskatchewan, forcing the western gentleman to quit in the eighth round. Fiddler is Western Cana-

dian champion. It was a non-title bout.

It was in the Fiddler fight that Richardson's hand injuries began, when he suffered a cracked bone in the third finger of his right hand. The hand injury put the Eastern Canada champion on the sidelines for almost four months.

1960 Bouts

Richardson started his 1960 campaign March 14, by stopping Dick Verde of Palmer, Mass. after

Fig. 6.6, 6.7. Pages from *Punching with Pemberton*. August 1962. Courtesy Rudy Plichie.

Following the Emery rematch, Richardson had three fights that he won by knockout. Emery and Richardson were then set to meet again for the rubber match in June, 1962.

More than 5,000 fans showed up in Halifax to see who would come away as the best fighter of the two. Because it wasn't a title bout, Richardson could only take the crown from Emery for Light Heavyweight Champion of Canada if he knocked him out. Richardson was the aggressor throughout the fight, pounding Emery with stinging lefts and a number of hard right crosses. At the end of ten, Emery was battered and bloodied but still standing. The judges had an easy decision in awarding the fight to Richardson, but he couldn't officially claim the national crown because Emery's experience and determination kept him on his feet as the final bell sounded. The local crowd went wild after Richardson's victory because they knew they had just witnessed one of the greatest boxers ever to come out of Nova Scotia, one of their own who was now within reach of a national championship.

Less than two months after sealing Burke Emery's fate, and unofficially becoming light heavyweight champion of Canada, Blair Richardson was given his first chance to officially win a national title. His opponent was Wilfie Greaves, an Albertan who was the reigning Canadian Middleweight Champion. The only other Cape Bretoners to formerly hold the national middleweight crown were Roddie "Big Pay" MacDonald from Glace Bay and George "Rockabye" Ross from West Bay. Richardson had big gloves to fill if he wanted to make it a trio of Cape Breton middleweight champs.

Wilfie Greaves had an early start in boxing when he was born sixty miles west of Edmonton, in the town of Entwistle; the minister who baptized him predicted that he would grow up to be a boxer. Sure enough, Greaves was wearing boxing gloves by the age of five, much to the displeasure of his mother. In an effort to dissuade him from the sport, she burned his first pair of gloves. But this didn't deter him. Greaves avoided schoolyard brawls as a boy and eventually turned to wrestling, as well. It was while watching the young Greaves wrestle one day that the boxing instructor Bob Ford decided he was strong enough to get serious about boxing. Greaves considered himself to be a poor loser who was also stubborn, and it was due in part to these less than desirable traits that he was drawn to boxing in order to let off steam. In the mind of the young Greaves, boxing made fighting legal. Greaves trained hard under Ford and eventually won a British Empire title in Vancouver as an amateur. The next year, 1955, he turned professional.[30]

A few years later, Greaves moved to Pittsburgh and made it his boxing home. He amassed twenty fights by the time he was granted a shot at the vacant Canadian Middleweight crown. His opponent was Cobey McCluskey, a tough middleweight from Prince Edward Island. On April 26, 1958, in Windsor, Ontario, Greaves took care of McCluskey with a knockout in the fourth round. Over the next few years, Greaves fought all of the top middleweights in the game. Eventually, he won and subsequently lost the British Empire title in two fights with Dick Tiger, the rugged Nigerian middleweight who twice was named (in 1962 and 1965) *Ring Magazine's* Fighter of the Year.

For the match-up between Greaves and Richardson, Gussie MacLellan guaranteed Greaves $3,500 and all expenses paid for a party of three to accompany him. Richardson was promised either $1,500 or 30 per cent of the gate, whichever was greater. MacLellan's biggest fear was that the Glace Bay Miners Forum wouldn't be able to hold everybody who wanted to witness the big fight. MacLellan said, "I've been deluged for days with requests for tickets. The requests have come from all over the Maritimes, with an especially heavy demand from Halifax."

Aubrey Keizer, writing in the *Cape Breton Post*, anticipated a large crowd of ex-patriate Cape Bretoners living in Halifax to make their way back across the causeway to see the fight because, "Blair is the golden boy up Halifax way." Keizer later wrote, "The Canadian Championship match has created the greatest interest in boxing in the Maritimes in a long time. Promoter Gussie MacLellan has extra police, ushers, ticket sellers and takers laid on for the big night."[31]

At age 21, and with 37 fights and only two losses in his pro career, Blair Richardson was ready for his run at the Canadian Middleweight Championship. Wilfie Greaves was no less confident. In the *Cape Breton Post*, he was quoted as saying, "I've come a long way and not to lose. I'm in top physical condition. I expect a tough fight and hope Richardson feels the same way. If he wants my title he'll have to win it."[32] Greaves's conditioning included a diet of high protein drinks, running two miles per day and avoiding cigarettes and booze.[33] Advance ticket sales for the fight were near the $10,000 mark, a smashing box office success for a relatively small market in 1962.

The stage was set and on July 28, before a packed crowd at the Glace Bay Miners Forum, Richardson and Greaves stepped into the ring. From the opening bell, it was evident to fans that Richardson was prepared to take the crown—and that Greaves was unwilling to give it up.[34]

Both fighters started off strong with Greaves more the aggressor, bringing the fight to the challenger. Richardson was rocked in the third but shook it off and, in fact, picked up the pace in the fourth. In that round, referee Bobby Beaton warned Greaves twice about throwing low blows. Leading with his jab, Richardson ruled the fifth but he was not hurting Greaves, who showed no signs of backing down. Greaves did slow somewhat in the sixth as Richardson continued to pepper him with jabs, but the eighth and ninth rounds were all Greaves as he began to pour on the punches to a visibly weakened Richardson. It was a long, tough battle but by the end of the nine rounds both judges and the referee had Richardson ahead on points. Only with a knockout could Greaves retain his title.

Those at ringside, however, realized that something didn't seem right with the blond slugger from South Bar. Between the ninth and tenth rounds, Richardson seemed almost out on his stool and his second had to lean against him to hold him up. As soon as Richardson got up for the start of the tenth round he was assailed by a flurry of punches from Greaves. He fell halfway through the ropes at one point, went to the mat on three occasions, and eventually staggered and fell. Before a shocked, open-mouthed crowd, Greaves got his knockout and kept his crown.

Though Richardson lost the fight and a chance at the Canadian championship, the fans and promoters on hand were not disappointed. It was a terrific fight and brought in a gate of more than $16,000 with 6,500 fans in attendance. The temperature inside the Miners Forum was over 100 °F and the place was thick with smoke. Richardson's manager, Johnny Buckley, was quoted in the *Cape Breton Post* as saying, "I've been in many important centers for championship fights but I've never seen one handled better than last night."

Following the fight, Richardson was quickly taken to hospital in Glace Bay to be examined. He claimed, "It was the heat. I ran out of steam and my legs went." It was later reported that Richardson was sick with a virus during the fight and had been weakened even more by trying to make weight by staying on a liquid diet. Though he suffered a tough loss to Greaves, Richardson knew he was not finished with the Albertan yet.

In *Halifax Champion*, Robert Ashe made the case that part of the reason Greaves won that fight was because Halifax promoter Clary Harris had sent trainer Tom McCluskey down to help Greaves and his team at the last minute.[35] Harris wanted to wrest control of Richardson from his regular promoter Gussie MacLellan and hoped a Richardson loss on his home turf would make MacLellan look bad.

Regardless of what extra-ring machinations went on, two months to the day, Richardson and Greaves were back at the Miners Forum before the same large and excited crowd for a rematch. The fight was originally planned for Halifax, where Richardson had fought many of his best bouts, but was switched to Glace Bay because the Halifax promoters wouldn't go for Richardson's 30 per cent gate demand. (Richardson was well known throughout the boxing community as having a good head for business as well as boxing. By agreeing on a percentage rather than a set $3,500 as Greaves did, Richardson the challenger earned more money on the fight—to the tune of $4,200—than the champion.)

On the days leading up to the rematch, both boxers were confident they would win. Richardson was in excellent condition and good health. He was being handled by Johnny Buckley again and had as his trainer the great

Freddy Brown, who had been trainer to both Rocky Marciano and Rocky Graziano. Both Buckley and Greaves's manager, C. W. Smith, were sure their boys would win. Cape Breton fans were anxious for Richardson to have his chance against "the nut buster," as Greaves became known locally for the low blows he had delivered in the first fight.

From the first round on, Richardson took command, throwing a barrage of jabs and hard rights, most of which connected.[36] Richardson took the second round, as well, but Greaves came back in the third. The third round had been going Richardson's way initially, Greaves had battled back. In the fourth, fans were on their feet as Greaves took a right to the jaw that spun him around and nearly floored him. Richardson had command of the following two rounds, bringing out his big right hand more than in any other round.

The battle was such a duel that the referee gave both fighters an extended five-minute break after the end of the sixth round. The extra rest wasn't enough time for Greaves to recuperate, though. Richardson was completely on the offensive and the only thing that saved Greaves in the seventh round was the bell. Richardson continued his onslaught, knocking Greaves down twice within the first thirty-three seconds of the eighth round before the referee called the match, awarding a TKO to Richardson. C. W. Smith himself signaled for the fight to end, saying afterwards, "Wilfie was in no condition to continue, that was obvious to all at ringside." By way of knockout, Blair Richardson, the handsome and humble gentleman from South Bar, was now Middleweight Champion of Canada. Fans went so wild after the victor was crowned that they swarmed into the ring and literally destroyed it.

Dave LeBlanc, former broadcaster and sports director with CJCB radio in Sydney, was just a thirteen-year-old boy when Richardson won the Canadian title that night. LeBlanc, who grew up in Glace Bay, remembers going to all of Richardson's fights when they were held in Glace Bay.

"Stevie 'The Kid' MacDonald, the former boxer, used to work the door at the Miners Forum taking tickets. We were just kids then going to see Blair's fights. We'd stick around the front waiting for the first punch to be thrown. Stevie would turn around to watch the fight and we'd be in. We had to be quick. We were only thirteen then and we didn't have any money to pay to get in. The Miners Forum was jammed back then. You couldn't even get in sometimes. It was all full of smoke. It was a real big deal. It was the heyday then for sure. We had five Canadian champions within two years of that win."[37]

As Aubrey Keizer wrote the next day in his column in the *Cape Breton Post*, "The Richardson victory was without question the most popular one in the Cape Breton ring in a long time. It reminded many fans of the days when George 'Rockabye' Ross was scaling the heights. Some can remember

Fig. 6.8
Gordie MacDougall and Karl Marsh (standing). Courtesy
Karl Marsh.

to the days of Roddie MacDonald and Jack McKenna."[38] Sports fan and
artist Karl Marsh, who drew excellent pictures of boxers over the years,
commented that this was a new and more determined Richardson who
tied up Greaves up on the inside and took command of the fight from the
opening bell with a stinging left jab and a thunderous right hand.[39]

Following Richardson's win over Greaves, fight promoters were quick
to get started on arranging a rubber match between the two middleweight
champs. Gussie MacLellan was also busy trying to arrange a fight between
Richardson and former World Welterweight Champion, Sugar Ray
Robinson, but that fight never came off. Richardson's next fight ended up
being against Vern LeMar in North Sydney.

Richardson went after LeMar with a flurry of punches in the first two
rounds. LeMar spent most of the fight trying to avoid getting hit until time
eventually ran out for him. And so Richardson rounded out 1962 by handily
defeating LeMar with a fourth round knockout. Blair Richardson then went
on to become the first Cape Bretoner to ever fight in New York's Madison
Square Garden.

Richardson's match in New York against world-ranked Joey Archer on
February 16, 1963, was also televised, which was another first for a Cape
Breton boxer. Few Cape Bretoners at that time had a television, but CJCB
radio carried the fight and thousands of eager fans at home were glued to
their radios.[40] Archer, after all, was about as good as they came. His career

record of 45-4 is somewhat misleading, as he lost the last three fights of his career, a career that included victories over the likes of Rubin "Hurricane" Carter (Carter became a political icon when he was wrongfully imprisoned for murder, and was later immortalized in song by Bob Dylan and on film by Norman Jewison) and Sugar Ray Robinson (Archer was the great Sugar Ray's last opponent). The final bout of Archer's career, in fact, was to be a highly controversial fifteen-round loss to World Middleweight Champion Emile Griffith. February 16, 1963, however, was not to be Richardson's night. While the fight went the distance, Archer was awarded a unanimous decision. Richardson did come breathtakingly close to putting Archer down in the ninth round, but it wasn't to be.

The Richardson loss was a tough pill to swallow for Maritime fight fans. As Archer was a highly ranked contender for the world title, many felt, and rightly so, that if Richardson had beaten him that night (and by all accounts, it was close) it would have put the Cape Bretoner in line for the biggest prize of them all—the middleweight world crown. In a letter to Earle Pemberton, Connecticut boxing promoter Pete Montesi had high praise for Richardson's style, saying that he had been a fan favourite, and was a big hit with the savvy fight crowd of New York City. Johnny Condon, the publicity director at the Garden stated: "There is nothing wrong with boxing that a few more Blair Richardson's can't cure. Boy, what an advertisement for the fight game."[41] Archer himself admitted Richardson hit him harder than he'd ever been hit before.[42]

Though Blair Richardson is best known in Cape Breton as a champion boxer, as early as 1963 he was also well onto a post-boxing career path that he also excelled at. Since he had spent a considerable amount of time training in the New England area, Richardson decided to start university there. He began taking courses at Boston University but soon transferred to Eastern Nazarene College. Richardson was from a Baptist family and had decided he was interested in becoming a minister. While studying at Eastern Nazarene, he lived with a minister's family for a while and led a high school bible studies group every Saturday morning.

Between his own course work and teaching bible studies to young people, Richardson also was disciplined enough to continue training for his third and final match against Wilfie Greaves. As soon as the college year ended, Richardson returned to Nova Scotia to take on Greaves on the night of May 4, in Halifax. It was a title match and Richardson had everything he strived for in boxing on the line. It had only been a few months since he'd taken the crown from Greaves and he wanted to retain it in order to eventually get a shot at the British Empire title.

It was a grueling match but the decision came out in the champion's favor. Greaves inflicted so many blows to Richardson's head in the later rounds that the Richardson camp feared that their fighter might have suffered internal

Fig. 6.9. Blair Richardson standing over Del Flanagan, referee Bob Beaton. Fans considered Flanagan an unworthy opponent for Richardson. June 1964. Abbass Studios Collection, Beaton Institute, Cape Breton University, B-2183b.

damage. After being declared the winner, Richardson was rushed to Victoria General Hospital for X-rays of his head. Though no serious injuries were found, this trip to the hospital may have foreshadowed Richardson's fate. Radio Broadcaster Pat Connolly described the three Richardson-Greaves fights as "the three most savage wars that I had ever seen in my life."[43]

Following his second victory over Wilfie Greaves, Richardson decided it was time to hang up the gloves for a while and devote more time to his studies. He returned to the United States and lived for some time with an aunt in Dorchester, Massachusetts. Though he was dedicated to his studies and his interest in religion, he still made time to keep an interest in boxing.

In June of 1964, Richardson returned to Cape Breton to take on Del Flanagan at the Glace Bay Miners Forum. Flanagan turned out to be one of the worst opponents—public-relations-wise—that Richardson had ever been paired up with. The *Cape Breton Highlander* gave an exceptionally colourful account of the fight.

"Cape Breton boxing took it on the chin Saturday night as Blair Richardson and Del Flanagan went through the motions in a putrid paunch fest promoted by Gus MacLellan. The affair was a bitter pill for the hope springs eternal fans, some of whom paid an incredible five dollars for a ringside view of the most superbly developed belly ever displayed in a Cape Breton ring.... The bout turned out to be a large nothing regarded as no contest by everybody but the boxing commission and the referee. Most fan reaction was confined to a chorus of boos that started with the unveiling of the Flanagan physique and continued until the farce was mercifully ended when Del slumped gracefully to the canvas. The immediate cause of his demise was not easily discernible to viewers but has been attributed variously to exhaustion, a Richardson punch, and even to fright.... When he finally folded, Del rolled onto his back, arms straight out and lay still while referee Bob Beaton tolled the fateful ten. Then looking suitably mollified, the corpulent St. Paul veteran donned his fresh white robe and faded away."[44]

In September, 1964, Richardson fought Joe DeNucci of Newton, Massachusetts. The fight was less a boxing match and more of a street fight with DeNucci doling out low blow after low blow while referee Bobby Beaton issued constant warnings for him to stop.[45] DeNucci actually injured Richardson due to such fouls in the seventh round and the fight was called off and awarded to Richardson. A rematch was held a few months later in the Miners Forum in Glace Bay in front of 5,000 cheering fans. Dave LeBlanc remembers the DeNucci fight as a tough one for Blair. "DeNucci was a rugged guy. He was chunky, a real battler," said LeBlanc. The fight went the full ten rounds.

Ace Foley wrote in the *Chronicle Herald* that "DeNucci started the fight as if he intended to blast the Cape Bretoner right out of the ring. Richardson came back and they often stood toe-to-toe, and the superior firepower of the South Bar belter became apparent as early as the fourth round." Richardson took some of DeNucci's best shots, but doled out far more than he took. According to writer Robert Ashe, Richardson had warned DeNucci prior to the fight that he wouldn't tolerate any funny stuff.[46] DeNucci didn't heed the warning and planted a fist into Richardson's groin early in the match. Richardson returned with "two stiff shots into DeNucci's crotch, opened cuts above DeNucci's eyes, sent him through the ropes twice, knocked him down once, and pounded his face into a puffy grotesque mask." The unanimous decision went to Richardson in what Ace Foley called, "probably the greatest fight of his fistic career."[47] DeNucci would years later declare Richardson a credit to boxing and to Canada.

With DeNucci out of his way, Richardson began to think more seriously about the British Empire Middleweight title that was still within his reach. Gomeo Brennan, a Bahamian who fought out of Miami Beach, Florida, was the current titleholder.[48] Brennan began his professional career in 1956, the same year as Richardson. He had fought an astounding eighteen fights that year, winning twelve, losing three and drawing three.

Throughout his career, Brennan was managed by Angelo Dundee, who later managed the great Muhammad Ali, and in the years leading up to his 1963 meeting with Richardson, Brennan had battled some of the best fighters in the game, from welterweights to light heavyweights, including top middleweight contender Rubin "Hurricane" Carter. Brennan lost a close ten-round decision to Carter in February, 1963, at Madison Square Garden.

In October, 1963, Brennan was given the opportunity to fight for the vacant British Empire Middleweight title. He fought the other top contender for the crown, Irish boxer Mick Leahy, in London, England. The fight went the distance—15 rounds—with the decision being awarded to Brennan. Five months later, in March, 1964, Brennan lost the title to the tough Samoan middleweight Tuna Scanlan in a 15-round bout held in Auckland, New Zealand. But in the topsy-turvy world of professional boxing, titles

Fig. 6.10. (Left to right): promoter Gussie MacLellan, Gomeo Brennan and Izzy Klein (Brennan's promoter). 1965. Abbass Studios Collection, Beaton Institute, Cape Breton University, B-4143a.

Fig. 6.11.
Gomeo Brennan's weigh-in, for British Empire middleweight championship against Richardson. (L-R): Glace Bay mayor Dan MacDonald, Brennan, Izzy Klein, Blair Richardson, Johnny Dan MacDonald and Andy MacDougall (boxing commissioners). 1966. Abbass Studios Collection, Beaton Institute, Cape Breton University, B-5062.

are often left vacant when a champion decides to retire with the crown, and as it happened, the British Empire title was available. Brennan promptly regained it by beating New Zealander Earl Nikora in a 15-round bout, also staged in Auckland. A rematch was held in March, 1965, and again the decision went to Brennan.

By 1965, Blair Richardson was well underway in his academic career, yet his passion for boxing had not waned. And since Brennan was running out of challengers in the southern hemisphere, his next move was to come north. On September 25, 1965, Gomeo Brennan and Blair Richardson met in Glace Bay at the Miners Forum for a 12-round title match for the British Empire Middleweight crown. Richardson fought hard but was unable to hurt the title-holder, who held on to his belt with an eleventh round knockout. [49]

Many former boxers and fight fans believe Brennan beat Richardson because he picked up on Blair's only weakness inside the ring, he'd stand up from the stool and pull his shorts up with his gloves. This split second of distraction was enough to let an opponent get a free shot in at the otherwise hard to hit Richardson. [50] Whatever the case, six months later Brennan was back in Glace Bay for a highly anticipated rematch.

Fig. 6.12. Blair Richardson (left) vs. Gomeo Brennan. First match for British Empire middleweight championship (successfully defended by Brennan. Sept. 1965. Abbass Studios Collection, Beaton Institute, Cape Breton University, B-4139.

The rematch was held on March 26, 1966. Over 4,000 fans showed up to see if their hometown boy could take the British Empire crown. At the time, the gate receipts totalling $24,000 were the biggest in Maritime boxing history. The bout was scheduled to go thirteen rounds, the first of its kind in a British Empire championship match. Cut man Rudy Plichie recalled that Richardson preferred a shorter fight of twelve rounds, whereas Brennan preferred a longer one.[51] Plichie noticed in the regulations that it said a championship fight had to be fifteen rounds or less. This rule, meant to cover the maximum rounds a fight could go, could also be interpreted to mean a fight could be scheduled for less. This technicality allowed the match to be set for thirteen rounds. Plichie thinks it was the first and last thirteen round fight held. For Blair Richardson, what mattered most was that the fight constituted the culmination of ten years of hard work, training and dedication coming to a head this very night—only one man stood in his way. And on fight night, Blair Richardson was up for the challenge. As nobly as he fought to retain his crown, Brennan ultimately ran out of steam and Richardson won by decision. The Cape Breton gentleman had at last achieved his goal. He was now British Empire Middleweight Champion, and suffice it to say, one of the best middleweights in the world.

Richardson returned to his studies and in June, 1967, announced he was retiring from boxing for good. In his ten-year career he had amassed a record of 46-5-2 with 36 knockouts. It's worth noting that Richardson won every rematch he fought.

Richardson went on to enter the ministry and by 1969 he was a professor at Northeastern University in Boston. That same year he married a young woman from Sydney Mines, Beverly Anne MacDowell. In the years

He spends Saturday nights directing youth activities, like this group from Tremont Temple Baptist Church.

Fig. 6.13.
Blair Richardson and young people in Boston. Clipping courtesy Whitney Pier Historical Society.

he participated in the sport, Blair Richardson exemplified the clean-living, clean-fighting boxer. He neither smoked nor drank, had the utmost respect for his opponents, and was a role model to a generation of young boxers that followed. As both teacher and preacher, he dedicated a considerable amount of time to travelling and doing outreach work with youth throughout the state of Massachusetts.

By the time Blair Richardson was thirty he was a retired middleweight champion boxer, a teacher, a preacher and a husband. He accomplished more in thirty years than most do in a lifetime. As a youngster he pitched a no-hitter with the Ward Six Indians in Little league and was a hard hitting defenceman who loved the heavy going in high school hockey. He helped the Sydney Academy juvenile team win the Maritime title in the late 1950s.[52] As a boxer with religion, the only problem he ever had with bible teachings dealt with "turning the other cheek."[53] For the humble pugilist from South Bar could never be accused of doing that in his boxing days. In fact, over the course of the final fights of his career, Richardson had begun to dislike the fact that he inflicted injury on his fellow man, and it was these feelings that ultimately aided in his decision to retire from the ring for good.

On March 5, 1971, in Boston, less than two months after his thirtieth birthday, Blair Richardson died as a result of what was reported to be a brain tumor. Cape Bretoners were devastated by this untimely tragedy. After working so long and hard to get where he was, it seemed almost impossible that Blair Richardson could be taken so early in life. It became even more difficult for his family and friends to bear when it became known that his wife, Beverly, was pregnant with their first child. People today still wonder if his years in the ring may have contributed to his early death. However, it was observed that another member of Richardson's family had suffered the same malady and fate as he did.

At the time of his death, Blair was a professor at Northeastern University and an instructor in the school's drama and speech department. He had also been working with the Ruggles Street Baptist Church in Boston as their athletic director and was hosting a religious themed radio program for youth in the Boston area. His wife told the media at the time of his death that her husband had started suffering severe headaches in December of the previous year. A kind and generous man to the end, just prior to his death Richardson awoke from a state of unconsciousness and asked that his kidneys be donated to two critically ill children.

Johnny Nemis, Richardson's first trainer and the man who recognized potential in the young blonde kid from South Bar when he first strolled into the Steelworkers gym in 1955, remarked that, "Blair Richardson was a hard-hitting, determined boxer who dedicated himself to achieving perfection in the sport to which he was dedicated. He was a credit to the sport and his untimely death is a harsh blow to boxing in Cape Breton."[54]

Don MacIsaac, president of Canadian Professional Boxing Federation and chairman of the Cape Breton Boxing Commission, said "He was a credit to boxing and his fine example in and out of the ring lifted boxing to the highest level the sport has ever known in Eastern Canada. Blair was respected by all for his marvelous courage. He fought the best of his time and won the admiration of all with his tremendous desire and ability. He never let down till he had given his all."

RICHARDSON MEETS DEMPSEY—Young Blair Richardson of South Bar, holder of the eastern Canada middleweight boxing title, received a big thrill when he met and chatted with the former world's heavyweight champion, Jack Dempsey, during the latter's recent Cape Breton visit. Above, Dempsey (right) is shown sparring with Richardson while his manager-trainer, Johnny Nemis, looks on. Richardson hopes to be ready to return to the ring next month. He has been sidelined with a fractured jaw and hand. (Abbass photo)

Fig. 6.14. Johnny Nemis, Blair Richardson and Jack Dempsey. Clipping courtesy Tyrone Gardiner.

Veteran referee Bobby Beaton remarked, "In his many fights there was never anyone who fought so clean and with more heart and determination than Blair. We all know how many times that, despite broken bones early in a bout, he still carried on to gain a victory." In the *Chronicle Herald*, Ian Donaldson stated Blair's 1967 decision to retire from boxing, "brought a virtual end to big gate boxing in this province, which prides itself on the number of Canadian champions it has produced. He was urged to make a comeback but declined."

Rather than continue with the sport he once loved, he chose his studies and his work with young people instead. In many ways, Blair Richardson's retirement from boxing and his subsequent untimely passing marked the beginning of the end for Cape Breton's rich and renowned boxing culture. After Blair Richardson, many would observe, things would never be quite the same again.

ROUND SEVEN:
ROCKY MACDOUGALL, FEATHERWEIGHT

By 1965, Sydney, Nova Scotia, the "Steel City," had a right to boast. With a population of just 33,000, Sydney had produced not one but two Canadian boxing champions—the lightweight Tyrone Gardiner and the middleweight Blair Richardson. In February of that year, in just his eighth professional bout, a young boxer out of Whitney Pier named Francis "Rocky" MacDougall won the vacant Eastern Canadian Featherweight title in a bout with Gil "Rocky" Boulay of Quebec City. According to veteran cut man Rudy Plichie, who'd been close to so many of Cape Breton's best boxers, MacDougall was a thrilling, quick-on-his-feet fighter, a fan favourite who never gave the crowd a dull moment.[1] And as was so prized in the lighter weight divisions—featherweights tipped the scales at just 126 lbs (57 kilos)—MacDougall had dynamite in both hands, true knockout power. Only two fighters MacDougall faced in his career had a higher knockout percentage and one of those, Dartmouth's Jackie Carter, was a natural lightweight. According to Plichie, MacDougall's punches had "the kick of a mule." He was, by all accounts, one of the hardest hitting featherweights that Canada—not just Cape Breton or the Maritimes—had produced up to that time.

Fig. 7.1. Francis "Rocky" MacDougall. 1960s. Photographer unknown. Courtesy Tyrone Gardiner.

Like many Cape Breton fighters of his day, MacDougall hailed from the boxing hotbed of Whitney Pier where he lived with his parents, Sylvine and Sadie MacDougall, two brothers and a sister.[2] "The first time I went into a boxing ring was the old local 1064 Steelworkers Union Hall that had a gym down below," MacDougall reminisced in 2007. "It was run by Johnny Nemis, Mick Conway and Walter "Boom

Boom" Gillis from Ingonish. I used to make the trek over from Tupper Street, walk the tracks and have my workout. I was around 14 years old around then, back in 1957, 1958."[3]

At first, MacDougall wasn't that serious about the sport and temporarily gave it up and went on to other things. But one day while the young MacDougall was walking home, a local boxing promoter stopped him. According to MacDougall:

"There were a couple of brothers boxing back then, twins, and one day Bill Talbot approached me and said, 'Would you like to box?' I said sure. I only had two amateur boxing matches up to then, over at the 1064 gym. I was in high school at the time. He asked me if I wanted to box professionally. I asked him what was involved and he said, 'If you box professionally you get paid.' For an amateur fight you'd get a trophy. I though this was a great idea. I wanted to box anyway and now I'd get paid for it. I went over to Johnny Cechetto's gym at the Venetian Gardens, but he was away in Italy at the time. Rudy Plichie was there and he got me involved. The first pro match I had at the Gardens was with a guy named Lloyd Parker and I knocked him out. In the meantime Johnny came over from Italy and took over my training. The next fight I fought Norman Parker, he was Lloyd's twin and I knocked him out too. They were from Leitches Creek."

MacDougall recalled that the Venetian Gardens wasn't a very big venue. "You couldn't get a lot of people in there so the cost of putting on a match wasn't that much. There were benches in there and people would line up all around. It was the old style fight venue and I can always remember there were no smoking rules and you were in there puffing the bad air and the good air. It was close knit and everybody was on top of each other. I was a small fighter, flyweight and bantamweight, in there."

Fight fan and former Sydney resident Melvin MacDougall, at 79 years of age, still has vivid memories of going to see the fights at the Venetian Gardens that echo Rocky MacDougall's recollections.

"You'd walk in there and hardly be able to see the ring for all the smoke. Everyone was smoking and some guys would have a mickey bottle in their pocket. The fighters would be in their best possible shape going in there to fight championship fights. It was like walking into a dungeon. That's the way to describe it. There were no chairs. Everyone was standing and smoking and the fighters would walk into that dungeon-like atmosphere. It was something else."[4]

After beating the Parker twins in the gloom of the Gardens, MacDougall's next fight pitted him against a somewhat more experienced opponent. Or at least, more experienced *looking*. MacDougall recalls the boxer was "a navy guy, covered with tattoos with a flattened nose." Says MacDougall, "I was a kid then and my face hadn't even been touched. I said to Johnny, 'That guy looks like a real fighter, look at his nose.' Johnny said back to me, 'Yeah look at his nose, he can be hit.' I thought that was great. From then on, every time I saw a guy with a flat nose I knew he could be hit. That was one of the things I remember from fighting someone I considered a real fighter."

MacDougall didn't consider himself a true fighter until after he fought the navy boxer. "Johnny used to tell me the whole idea of boxing was going in there and not getting hit. I won that fight easy. Bang, that was it." After this introduction to the world of professional boxing, Sydney style, MacDougall began to get more fights, most of which he won. Eventually, he worked his way up to fighting on the bigger cards staged at the Glace Bay Miners Forum. "I always thought the trip in to the Miners Forum from Sydney was terrific because there would always be a big line of cars one behind the other, and they were all heading for the Forum," recalls MacDougall. "As a young fellow, boxing at the Miners Forum was something else. Blair Richardson would be there and Tyrone Gardiner. And then coming home would be the same thing."

Cape Breton boxers had a long tradition of boxing in Boston, especially during the 1960s when Blair Richardson was living there, so it wasn't long before the young MacDougall made his way into the New England ring. MacDougall had fond memories of boxing in Boston, and of how the Cape Bretoners were welcomed by the Boston fight community.

"I can remember one time we were fighting in Boston and Johnny Cechetto, my manager, was with me, and Johnny always wore his hat on an angle, wore the suit, and had a big cigar and he looked like a typical promoter. He spoke broken English with an Italian accent and they got right off on him in Boston. They'd ask me who my trainer was and I say that's the guy right there. These guys (Gussie MacLellan, Johnny Cechetto) were real characters, they didn't play the part, they were genuine. That was them. If you had a movie today you'd be trying to get people to play their part. They were just characters. Johnny Nemis was the same way. He had things coming out of his mouth that would just flabbergast you. They were all very colorful people. In this day and age you don't have that."

By 1965, the young slugger from Whitney Pier had eighteen professional fights under his belt and Cechetto could feel that his boy was ready for a shot at a national title. In the fall of that year the opportunity came. Dave Hilton, whose four sons—Matthew, Dave, Jr., Alex and Stewart—would all become professional boxers, was reigning Canadian champ but he had failed to make his weight. According to the rules, the featherweight crown was thus declared vacant. The two top contenders at the time were MacDougall and twenty-four-year-old Marcel Bellefeuille of Montreal, a former Olympian.

The fight was staged at the Venetian Gardens on October 22, 1965, with a huge crowd on hand to see if MacDougall had the stuff to win the Canadian title.

Bellefeuille began his attack in the very first round with a hard blow to the body that appeared to hurt MacDougall. And so it had. Another hard body blow from Bellefeuille just seconds later and suddenly MacDougall was down on the canvas. He was back on his feet at a count of four but had to wait out the mandatory eight count before the fight could resume. Bellefeuille came right back at him, concentrating his attack on the body with a series of quick lefts that kept the now disoriented MacDougall off balance. To make matters worse, MacDougall kept missing with his own jab and so couldn't manage to set Bellefeuille up for his big right.

At the opening of the third round, Bellefeuille caught MacDougall again, this time with another hard right to the body. Though clearly shaken by the blow, MacDougall nevertheless responded with a flurry of his own. He drove the Frenchman into the ropes with a hard right lead and then a brace of lefts that sent Bellefeuille reeling. Now it was Bellefeuille's turn to wait out the eight count. When the round was allowed to resume,

Fig. 7.2. Rocky MacDougall (left) vs. Marcel Bellefeuille. 1965. Abbass Studios Collection, Beaton Institute, Cape Breton University, B-4288a.

MacDougall went at Bellefeuille hard, unleashing a flurry of punches that prompted referee Beaton to step in with another standing eight count for the wobbling Frenchman. Beaton had counted out seven when the bell sounded to end the round. Saved by the bell, Bellefeuille would now have a minute's reprieve on his stool to try to recover and get back in the fight.

As the fourth round got under-way it appeared that Bellefeuille was still in trouble, but then he surprised everyone, especially MacDougall and perhaps even himself, when he connected with a right to MacDougall's jaw that sent the hometown boy to the mat again. MacDougall took until a count of nine to make it back on his feet, and though it appeared the tide had turned in the Montrealer's favour, MacDougall was able to hang on and actually finish the round with a flurry of his own that saw Bellefeuille on the ropes, struggling to ward off blows. Yet, amidst the flurry, the Frenchman managed to connect with a right that nearly put MacDougall down again. And so it went, back and fourth, to and fro, through four dynamic and unpredictable rounds, with the packed house going wild.

MacDougall came out strong in the fifth and went on to own the round, forcing another standing eight count. Again, as in the third round, the badly shaken Bellefeuille was saved by the bell. In the sixth, it soon became evident that for the third time a Cape Bretoner would win a national title. MacDougall sent Bellefeuille to the canvas three times in the round, and with the "Three Knockdown Rule" in effect, at 2:15 of the sixth round referee Bobby Beaton called the fight and awarded a technical knockout—and the Canadian Featherweight Championship—to South Bar slugger Rocky MacDougall. It was now official: The Cape Bretoner was now the best fighter in his weight class in the country.

Sydney now had three national champions across three weight divisions, each of whom had risen up from sweaty, makeshift basement gyms and converted bingo halls to rule their sport on the national stage. For the record books, in 1965 three Canadian champions—Rocky MacDougall, Tyrone Gardiner and Blair Richardson—had all, at one time or another, trained out of Sydney. In boxing circles, such a concentration of world-class fighters was an accomplishment that was unheard of, especially when you take into account Sydney's modest population of just 33,000 souls.

At the time of his Canadian Championship victory, MacDougall was also studying at Xavier College. He continued his studies after winning the title and also kept up his training, and in March, 1966, MacDougall took on Hector Rodriguez of Boston at the Glace Bay Miners Forum, the same night that Blair Richardson won the British Empire Middleweight Crown.

Fig. 7.3. Rocky MacDougall in victory celebration, Venetian Gardens. (Left to right): Rudy Plichie, referee Bob Beaton, MacDougall, John Cechetto. 1965. Abbass Studios Collection, Beaton Institute, Cape Breton University, B-4288b.

The Rodriguez fight was a more or less see-saw battle, with neither fighter seeming to take control and with neither even willing to get into the bout and mix it up. In the fifth round of what had become something of a yawner, referee Gordie MacDougall actually had to step in and encourage the fighters to get more into it. According to a report on the fight in the *Cape Breton Post*, "Rodriguez went into action and struck three consecutive overhand rights to MacDougall's head. The last blow sent MacDougall to the canvas on one knee with six seconds remaining in the round." MacDougall, however, was able to battle back, taking the sixth and seventh rounds from the New England slugger and ultimately winning a split decision, though many in the audience felt it could have gone the other way.

In June, 1966, MacDougall put his championship crown on the line. His opponent was nineteen-year-old Billy McGrandle of Edmonton, Alberta. McGrandle came from a fighting family of four boys. His family had moved to Alberta in 1957 from Scotland, and his father soon had all the boys involved in boxing. His father John "Scotty" McGrandle, an amateur boxer of some note back home in Scotland, taught his boys to become clever fighters at an early age. Billy fought his first fight at age eleven and never looked back. He won numerous Golden Glove awards, boxed in the Pan American Games in Saskatchewan, and was Flyweight Champion of Canada in 1963. In 1964, McGrandle was selected for the Canadian Olympic Boxing team, but never went to Tokyo because of a minor police record.

The title bout was held on June 6, 1966, in Edmonton and went the full twelve rounds. Described as a grueling clutch-and-grab affair, MacDougall used every trick in the book but according to Aubrey Keizer in the *Cape Breton Post,* the champion had the crown "rocked from his head."[5] Keizer postulated, "The question arises, and it has often times, whether a fighter can fight and study. Well it has been asked in the Blair Richardson case, and Blair admits that he didn't have the same concentration when he was fighting and studying. Could be the same in the case of Rocky, who was finishing out a year at Xavier College when the Edmonton fight came up." Whether MacDougall was prepared or not for the title defense, fans in Edmonton were satisfied they'd seen a great fight, and a rematch, which was already arranged if MacDougall were to lose, was quickly set up. McGrandle's father was quoted as saying, "We have the right to have it here and we have the support of the crowd to warrant it here." And so the rematch would be held in, for MacDougall, the unfriendly environs of Edmonton.

The second MacDougall-McGrandle fight was held in Edmonton on August 2, 1966. The title defence went McGrandle's way though it was a close match. The decision was unanimous in the young Edmonton fighter's favour

Fig. 7.4. Three champs: Rocky MacDougall, Blair Richardson and Tyrone Gardiner, with trainer Johnny Cechetto. 1965. Abbass Studios Collection, Beaton Institute, Cape Breton University, B-4450a.

although MacDougall only lost by seven points, with the fight point total being 170-163 in favour of McGrandle. Not to be dissuaded by a swollen nose, McGrandle got married the day after the fight, while MacDougall returned to Cape Breton to ponder his boxing future. In 2007, a reminiscent MacDougall said his toughest fights were those against the Edmontonian Billy McGrandle.[6]

Over the next few years, Rocky MacDougall got married and concentrated on his studies more than boxing, though the urge to lace up the gloves and get his crown back from McGrandle never went away. By 1968, McGrandle was still Featherweight Champion of Canada and still defending his crown to the delight of his fans in Alberta. Both fighters and their respective promoters realized a third title fight between the two would be a big draw anywhere it was held, and eventually Regina, Saskatchewan, was chosen as the site. Saskatchewan Promoter Nick Zubray set it up as a double Canadian Championship card, with George Chuvalo defending his heavyweight crown against Jean Claude Roy as the headliner.

Fig. 7.5.
Cut man Rudy Plichie, Rocky MacDougall and trainer John Cechetto. May 25, 1966. Photo by Raytel. Courtesy Ray Doucette.

According to *The Leader-Post* of Regina, the upcoming Zubray card was considered to be an "outstanding event" that would stop the series of "bad luck breaks" he'd had in some previous Western Canadian promotions.[7] MacDougall arrived in Regina in late May, 1968, and started training at the Laird Gym under the watchful eye of his long time trainer Johnny Cechetto. Though Cechetto had announced his retirement from training in June, 1967, the opportunity to win the crown back with MacDougall was simply too tempting and served to bring him back to the game.[8]

Unfortunately for Nick Zubray, the prospect of an outstanding event that would have fights fans in Regina clamoring for tickets soon began to fall apart. McGrandle, as most Cape Breton boxers also did, held down a job while training and boxing. A few days after MacDougall came to town, McGrandle had acid splashed in his eye in an accident at work. Though he had actually fought and won a fight the night after his accident, McGrandle suffered an eye injury that doctors claimed would sideline him for at least two weeks, meaning the title fight against MacDougall would not be able to go forward. The Western Canadian newspapers were full of speculation as to whether McGrandle would fight or not. It appeared that not only the eye injury, but also contractual problems may have played a role in McGrandle's opting out of the MacDougall title challenge.[9] Billy McGrandle's father, Scotty, who was his trainer as well, claimed he had signed a contract for the fight, while a group out of Edmonton headed by Mitch Klimove claimed that *they* were the rightful managers of the younger McGrandle and that they did not sanction the fight. Reports out of Edmonton claim that Klimove eventually gave his consent for the fight but described it as "sheer lunacy" because of McGrandle's eye injury and the risk of causing greater damage.[10] According to Klimove, McGrandle wanted the fight to go on out of loyalty to promoter Nick Zubray. In the end, though, the fight never happened. To this day, Rocky MacDougall wonders about what really happened to make McGrandle pull out like he did.

Not long after Rocky MacDougall returned home, disappointed at not getting the chance to take back his Featherweight crown, the Canadian Professional Boxing Federation stripped McGrandle of the title. The fact that McGrandle was reported as having left Regina for Edmonton without giving the local boxing commission word he wouldn't be fighting MacDougall may have played a role in the national body's rationale for separating fighter from crown. With the title now vacant, a championship match was quickly arranged between MacDougall and Canadian Bantamweight champion Jackie Burke of Saint John, New Brunswick.

Trainer Johnny Cechetto was happy to have MacDougall go up against Burke because he felt an earlier Burke victory over his boy wasn't the right decision. Burke had recently returned from Edmonton where he had fought and beat MacDougall's nemesis, Billy McGrandle. Many local fight speculators felt this victory would give Burke the edge over MacDougall. The fight was set for September 17, 1969, at the Sydney Forum and was the first title match of the year to be held in Cape Breton. To the delight of his trainer, Johnny Cechetto, and his legions of fans, Rocky MacDougall proved he could still throw a punch. The victory went his way with a technical knockout in the eleventh round. For the second time in his career, Rocky MacDougall was the Featherweight Champion of Canada.

Fig. 7.6 Jackie Burke vs. Les Gillis. Photographer unknown. Courtesy Rudy Plichie.

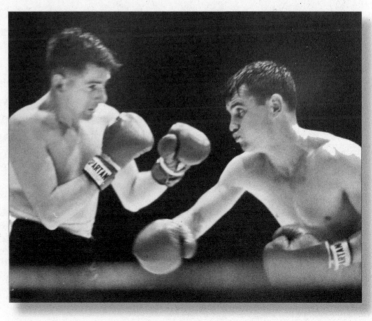

Over the next year-and-a-half, MacDougall continued his winning ways, defeating, among others, Fernand Durelle, nephew of Yvon Durelle, in a hard fought ten-round unanimous decision at the Glace Bay Miners Forum. MacDougall also fought fellow Cape Bretoner Les Gillis, Canadian Junior Lightweight Champion at the time.[11] Gillis was a New Waterford native and was the fourth Cape Bretoner to hold a national crown in the years spanning 1965-66. MacDougall had fought Gillis only once before, in 1963, and had won. Ever since that time a rivalry had developed not only between the two fighters but also amongst their loyal fans. The MacDougall-Gillis non-title grudge match went the distance in front of close to 2,000 fans at the Sydney Forum with Gillis coming out on top.

In June of 1971, the fight Rocky MacDougall had really wanted in1968 finally came about. Billy McGrandle, who had been in retirement for about eighteen months, decided to give it another go. Upon arriving in Halifax for the title fight, which would be held on July 1, 1971, McGrandle was quoted in the *Chronicle Herald* as saying about his early start in boxing, "I was pushed into it.... My Dad used to fight and therefore it was a foregone conclusion I would fight."[12] McGrandle felt he was in excellent shape and the two months of training he'd done before getting to Halifax would be enough to win back the featherweight title from MacDougall.

Writing about the fight afterwards, Ken Jennex stated, "McGrandle was taunting in the first four rounds. Then midway through the fifth round MacDougall landed a stiff left hook on the bridge of McGrandle's nose. McGrandle's face was smeared with blood from his broken nose."[13] The broken nose not only turned on the red tide for McGrandle, it turned the tide for MacDougall. The fight went the distance and the Canadian champion from Cape Breton retained his crown.

In 1972, less than a year after regaining and defending the Canadian Featherweight Championship, Rocky MacDougall retired. In his professional career he had fought forty-two times, losing only five bouts. MacDougall recalls the days after he hung up his gloves for good.

"I was married, had a family and was living in Antigonish. I finished my Business degree. Then I got a Bachelor of Education and started teaching. While I was doing that I started coaching and refereeing. I went all over the world as an official. I went to a Pan American games, two Commonwealth games, and two Olympic games. I went to Italy and Cuba for the World Junior Championships...."

Rocky MacDougall spent a few years working in a bank until he got his teaching degree. During this time he and his wife Beverly had three children, Sean, Stacey and Jody. He spent twenty-seven years teaching elementary school before he retired. For a two-time Canadian Featherweight Champion, a career as an elementary school teacher is quite the contrast to that of professional boxer. Like Blair Richardson, Tyrone Gardiner, and many other Cape Breton boxers of his era, MacDougall exhibited a duality of person. One the mighty boxing hero, the other a kind, erudite and modest individual willing to help anyone in need. MacDougall described this notion as such:

"It's interesting that boxers can have two sides to their personality. There's that gentle side of Blair Richardson then there's that other side of him who was the fighter in the ring. It was often said of myself when I was fighting that I had two sides. This Harris guy from the *Chronicle Herald* perceived me like that. There was the banker dressed in the suit who didn't look like I could lick my lips, then I'd leave that and go into the ring and be the Featherweight Champion of Canada. These two sides were always tugging at each other. Most boxers are very gentle people."

These same sentiments about the dual nature of a boxer are still alive and well in Cape Breton today. Mi'kmaw boxer Jaime Battiste of Eskasoni boxed in 2006 and 2007 as a heavyweight while lecturing at Cape Breton University in Mi'Kmaq studies and Aboriginal treaty rights. Once in the ring you become a different person he says. "It's always exciting, but it's always nerve wracking at the same time."[14]

Rocky MacDougall remained involved with boxing on the local scene as a referee up until 2008 when he was stricken by cancer. A number of his close friends including Blair Joseph and Tyrone Gardiner staged a benefit in 2009 on his behalf to raise money to pay for his expensive medication. Close to 400 people attended the event to celebrate the life of one of their local heroes. MacDougall and his wife Beverly attended the benefit and he was in excellent spirits and looked terrific considering his once mighty body was being ravaged by disease. A few weeks later he was seen perusing photographs of boxers in the Beaton Institute Archives at Cape Breton University. Shortly after that he passed away at his home in Antigonish. As he once said, "Boxing has been good to me and I really loved it, and I still do." And his fans, of which there were and remain many—they still love him too.

Fig.7.7.
Rocky MacDougall, Ronnie Sampson and trainer John Cechetto. Photographer unknown. Courtesy Tyrone Gardiner.

Rocky MacDougall & Ronnie Sampson & John Cechetto

ROUND EIGHT: FIGHTING, DRINKING, LIVING AND DYING
GORDIE MACDOUGALL

For those few boxers who were born and trained in Cape Breton and who went on to achieve championship status on the national stage—often from humble beginnings that involved cutting wood, mining coal or making steel—there were dozens more fighters who could also have been champs—the skill, the work ethic, the gifts were there— if only the lights that shone down on the ring, and the spirits that surround it, had aligned for them. Gordie MacDougall of South Bar was one such boxer.

Gordie MacDougall, who helped Blair Richardson learn how to dance around the ring

Fig. 8.1.
Gordie MacDougall.
Courtesy Karl Marsh.

in his early days, fought a total of fifty-six fights in his ten-year career, losing only four times. According to Rudy Plichie, "Gordie could have gone all the way, if the champions would have gave him the opportunity to fight for either the middleweight or light heavyweight titles."

While MacDougall is remembered today for his boxing prowess, he was also an excellent baseball player as well as a track and field star. In

1959, as a pitcher, he helped the New Waterford Giants win the first of two Nova Scotia senior baseball championships. Prior to getting into boxing, MacDougall was a runner. He was good enough that on several occasions he beat Glace Bay's Joey Mullins, who was one of the best sprinters of his day. In 1956, Mullins set a world indoor record for the 600-yard run; and in 1960, he was an Olympian at the summer games in Rome. Keeping such company, in not just one sport but several, speaks to the athletic prowess of the young Gordie MacDougall.

In the early 1990s, MacDougall spoke at length about his boxing career and his life in general to *Cape Breton's Magazine* interviewers. His interest in boxing began when he was around eleven years old. He had a pair of gloves and used to challenge other neighbourhood kids to fights in his father's barn. MacDougall would usually send them home with black eyes and bloody noses and have to bribe them with candy to come back the next time to get beat again. He was a tough kid at school, too, always getting in fights

Fig. 8.2. Blair Richardson posing with Gordie MacDougall. 1960. Abbass Studios Collection, Beaton Institute, Cape Breton University, A-6226.

with other kids. "It was a wonder I wasn't killed or punch drunk," he says, "because all the kids used to pound me."[1]

Like Tyrone Gardiner's father, MacDougall's father didn't like the idea of his son getting involved in boxing. The young puncher returned home one day to learn from his mother that his father had thrown all his boxing gear into the furnace. MacDougall would eventually earn enough money collecting and returning beer bottles to buy some secondhand gloves and gear to replace the stuff that had gone up in smoke at his father's hand. His father's dislike of boxing never diminished. He refused to go to any of his son's matches, no matter how successful Gordie became in later years.

Local fight fan Stan McPhail was with Gordie MacDougall the first time the young fighter entered a boxing ring.

"Gordie had to sneak away from his father, Russell, because if he found out he was going to go boxing he would have killed him! Russell was a tough old rugby player who played for Caledonia and sported a twisted nose. Well Gordie and I went to the Venetian Gardens and he wasn't there that long sparring when guys asked where did this guy come from. He was a natural fighter. He was a runner, and baseball player for New Waterford, too."[2]

MacDougall's mother, as it turned out, wasn't as opposed to his boxing as his father. McPhail recalls that she used to make bandages for her son and put them in his coat pocket when he went out to the gym.

Low Point and South Bar are tiny communities that line the coastal road between Sydney's Whitney Pier district and the neighbouring town of New Waterford. Down at Low Point there was a hall that was frequented by some of the boxers of the area. MacDougall remembers going there for

Fig. 8.3. Ernie MacKinnon. Clipping from *Cape Breton's Magazine*. Courtesy Paul MacDougall.

Ernie MacKinnon

the first time with his high school friend—and boxing *protégé* of Johnny Nemis—Ernie MacKinnon. "[MacKinnon] was a heck of a good fighter. He was fighting at the time. So he used to ask me to go down to the hall down by his place, down Low Point," said MacDougall. "We'd put an old alarm clock on the chair. Only two of us in the hall. We'd set the alarm clock to go off in maybe three minutes, some rounds would be five. And we'd box. He kept after me, 'Come on. Come on to the gym with me.' So then I finally said, 'Yeah, okay, I'll go to the gym with you'."

MacDougall was getting into a lot of "mischief" then, as he called it, and was known by police to be troublesome. The police would often refer kids like Gordie to the Police Club gym run by Johnny Nemis. For the police, the gym was a way to keep kids off the streets and out of trouble, as well as a way to keep an eye on them. Johnny Nemis was training Ernie MacKinnon at the time and many Sydney fight fans felt that MacKinnon represented Johnny's last chance to go the distance and train a champion—a feat that, despite his years in the fight game, Nemis had never achieved.

Though Nemis was a crucial trainer to young boxers on the way up, he had never got the chance to deliver the goods, which is to say, he had never taken a fighter all the way to a national title. In fact, an almost natural progression for young Cape Breton fighters at the time was to start out with Johnny Nemis and finish with John Cechetto. But in the young Gordie MacDougall's day, local fight fans felt—hoped—that Johnny Nemis had a future champion in Ernie MacKinnon.

Cape Breton University professor Richard MacKinnon, a nephew of Ernie MacKinnon, recalls how boxing came natural to the MacKinnon clan. "Everyone was into boxing back then," he recalls.

"It was nothing for a bunch of guys to come over to our place and go down into the basement, strap on the gloves and go a few rounds with each other. My brother and I would come upstairs with bloody noses and be all banged up and nobody would cast a glance. Imagine that today. Parents would get all upset now if you had a bleeding nose from deliberately fighting with a friend."[3]

Richard MacKinnon states that as far as he can remember the only person ever to knock out his uncle Ernie was his uncle Ernie's father, and occasionally, Ernie's older brother Francis. "That was always the story at our house," says Richard, thinking back. "Dad was the only person who ever knocked out Ernie."

Retired city of Sydney assessor and fight fan Charlie Hopkins also remembers Ernie MacKinnon. "Ernie was sure-fire material back then. He could hit and he had lots of movement. I don't think I ever saw him take a backwards step. He was a heck of a fighter and a nice boy."[4] Hopkins remembers one MacKinnon fight in particular. "I saw him fight on the night he graduated from Sydney Academy high school. He took off all his gear, the tuxedo and all that. He went in and won his fight. The fight only lasted a round or a round and a half. Then he went back to the graduation dance. He hadn't even worked up a sweat."

Ernie MacKinnon was quickly becoming known in Cape Breton boxing circles. Part of his fast rise in reputation and popularity among fans lay in the fact that MacKinnon typified, for many, what boxing was all about. He had fierce drive and determination, and these qualities struck a chord with not just fans but with other boxers. Tragically, Ernie MacKinnon never got the chance to prove how good a boxer he could be. He was killed in a single car accident on the South Bar road while returning home after a night working in the coal mine. He had just turned professional after having gone undefeated in his amateur career. Ernie MacKinnon was only nineteen years old. According to Charlie Hopkins and many others, "He could have been one of the best."

It may be said that while the untimely death of Blair Richardson knocked the wind out of Cape Breton's boxing community, the death of Ernie

MacKinnon, eleven years earlier represented the community's first serious blow. As a shocked and saddened community learned of MacKinnon's tragic end, it became immediately evident to everyone that the young fighter's death took the joy out of the boxing game for Johnny Nemis from that point on. People could tell he just wasn't the same. Gordie MacDougall, however, took the death of his closest friend another way.

"That kind of set us, me and Johnny Nemis, back quite a bit. I lost one of the best friends I ever had in Ernie MacKinnon. So I laid off boxing for six months or so. Then I started her up again real sincere, more or less on Ernie's behalf, you know. So, things steamrolled from there."

And so they did. After MacKinnon's death, Gordie MacDougall began to take the sport of boxing more seriously, his friend's memory inspiring him and spurring him on. (As a gesture of honour and remembrance, MacDougall would name a future son after his fallen friend.) In addition to training, MacDougall worked in the woods as a lumberjack, which helped to toughen him up and keep him sharp. "I used to spar at least five or six rounds a day, say five days a week. You took more punishment in training then you did sometimes in an actual fight," recalled MacDougall.

Walter MacPhail remembers sparring with MacDougall two days before Gordie was to box a fighter going by the handle of Beau Jack. "He hit me so hard while sparring I had a headache that lasted for two days, said MacPhail. "This made me so mad I came back out swinging and knocked him out. Johnny Nemis never asked me to spar with Gordie again and there was no love lost between Gordie and I since then. He ended up loosing to Jack as well. Johnny told me afterwards all Beau could afford to eat was hotdogs, if he ate steak he'd beat everyone in his weight class."[5]

Though he took many lumps in the ring as well as while sparring, MacDougall loved to fight and was never shy about saying it. "The tougher the fights were, the better I loved it. Some of them were real wars, they were real tough. God, you went home after a fight, your face was pretty sore." Boxers today worry too much about their facial features, according to MacDougall. He recalls that in his day the nose was the focal point of all the punches. Once it got broken there was no sense fixing it, MacDougall reasoned, because you'd just get it broken again.

By the time MacDougall was into his career as a professional boxer he had developed a reputation as a fighter with a hard, snapping jab that could hit you from any angle.[6] He fought a number of good boxers in the area, many who far outweighed him, but who he could outmaneuver with upper body and head movements that took him beyond their reach. However, for all his boxing skills, he never got a shot at a title. Looking back, MacDougall describes his disappointment with the winding path that was his career.

BENNY DELORENZO
Boxer

Birth Place: Sept. 23, 1926, at Sydney, N.S.
Boxing Record: Combined, Amateur, Pro 106 fights, Won 93, Lost 7, Draw 6
Height: 5 ft. 5 in. — Campaigned in Weights from 118 lbs. to 135 lbs.

RING STYLE:
Smooth and classy stylist extremely clever, very popular performer — Benny a product of the Golden Glove's era. He won many regional, maritimes, eastern "Canada" titles, when the competition was at a high level during 1940's and 1950's.

Benny would draw fans from all over the Maritimes, when his name appeared on Amateur and Professional Boxing Card's.

After Benny retired, Boxing being his first love — he opened a Gym. He was always available to give the youth the benefit of his experiences.

He was a credit to the Boxing "Game", here in Canada. Benny has a great interest in all youth sport movements in the community.

GORDIE MACDOUGALL
Boxer

Birth Place: June 15th, 1934, South Bar, Cape Breton
Boxing Record: Total 56 fights, Won 50, Lost 4, Drew 2
Height: 5 ft. 9½ ins.
Weight: 160-165 lbs.

RING STYLE:
Boxer Puncher set up big right hands with a snapping jab, could attack from any angle. Never fought floor competition — often his opponent outweighed him by 25 lbs. He'd outmaneuver the heavy fighter. With upper body and head movement he could twist away from punches; that way he passed by many good fighters in Canada. When the opposition got slack in eastern Canada he joined the fighting Stable of the Irish

Fig. 8.4. Gordie MacDougall. *The Unitas Boxing News.* Clipping courtesy Hilton Smith.

"Well, you were promised fights. If you fought this fellow and you won they'd promise you a shot at the Canadian champion. So you fought the guy. Then you were waiting for that big shot. Then they'd give you a runaround, the promoter or the manager of the other fighter'd give you the runaround. Instead of signing to fight you he'd sign to fight somebody else. Sidestep you. You know, you got kicked around a lot."

MacDougall was an anxious fighter who firmly believed that to be a good boxer you had to fight every couple of weeks or so. "I think a young kid should be fighting every two weeks. That's the only way of keeping him sharp, for him to learn his trade. You box often, you keep yourself sharp." MacDougall claimed that fighting often meant he'd be around better fighters and thus learn from them. When MacDougall had had enough with the lack of fight opportunities in the Maritimes he decided, like many other Cape Breton boxers before him, to give it a shot States-side.

MacDougall moved to Minnesota and was based out of Minneapolis for a couple of years. He boxed in St. Paul, Kansas City, St. Louis, Butte, Omaha, even California. In the time he spent in the States, Gordie MacDougall met world champion boxers and celebrities that most young men his age would only ever dream of meeting. He met Jack Dempsey and Sugar Ray Robinson; he saw Archie Moore and Floyd Patterson fight for the world heavyweight title in 1956 at Chicago Stadium. "I was at their training camp," he recalled. MacDougall was also granted access to watch Rocky Marciano train. In California, MacDougall rubbed shoulders with the legendary "Rat Pack" of Frank Sinatra, Sammy Davis Jr., Shirley McLaine and Peter Lawford. MacDougall recalled, "See, they were all fight fans. I was only fighting six-rounders out there, but I was with Del Flanagan, Al Andrews, those guys. They were fighting main events, the top fighters in the world. I was out with them. I was a sparring partner." The 19-year-old self-professed "dumb cluck from Cape Breton," who was hobnobbing with the likes of Frank Sinatra at lavish country club parties, seemed destined for greatness.

Though MacDougall proclaims to have had a wonderful life it appears his early years were besot by hard times due to reasons even MacDougall couldn't fully explain, save for not fighting often enough and not getting paid enough per fight. MacDougall says that often the hard times involved his getting discouraged with the way the fights were arranged and who got to fight who. Unfortunately for MacDougall, bouts of discouragement often led to bouts with the bottle.

"I had some hard times and I just happened to drift into that life. Discouragements.... In the boxing game and with jobs, too. It was a number of different things. You know, I just thought the world is tumbling down on you, you know what I mean? And I said 'Aw, Jesus.' And you think out of the mouth of a bottle. It solves everything. And the more you drank the more carefree you got. And you forgot all your troubles."

MacDougall's drinking habit took control of his life and took him down to the very bottom. At the worst of times, he would drink just about anything he could get his hands on. Anything that had a sniff of alcohol in it. Vanilla extract by the bottle, shaving lotion, even perfume. Nothing was off limits to the men on Sydney's skid row in the 1950s and 1960s. MacDougall remembers walking up Charlotte Street one day with other heavy drinkers. "This guy, it was his turn to go into the store to steal some shoe polish. The paste shoe polish. You'd melt that down." MacDougall remembers one of the old-timers saying, "Get anything but that Nugget [brand] ... that Nugget gives me heartburn!"

One of the hangouts for hard drinkers and others down on their luck at the time was around the railway track or underneath the coal trestle behind the Sydney Forum. Local lumber shacks were also a welcome haunt. MacDougall describes how he and his drinking partners used to melt down old 78 record albums when they had absolutely nothing else to drink. He claimed he'd had more Bing Crosby tunes in him than Bing himself from drinking so many melted down records.

"We used to go through the garbage around the city. People had broken records they'd throw out in the garbage. So we used to pick them all up. There's alcohol in records. So we used to go and take a pot and we'd go down by the railway tracks and we'd boil the records and strain them through cheesecloth into a pot. And we'd drink it out of a pot. It gave you a hell of a bang after you drank so many of those records. And then you went loony tunes down the street."

Somehow, MacDougall was able to battle back from these depths. Still in his twenties, he got himself in shape enough to return to cutting wood for a living. He'd given up on boxing for at least a year-and-a-half and had two kids and a wife to support. MacDougall was living in East Bay when one day Benny Gaum drove up in a big Cadillac. Gaum was a fight promoter from Sydney who some say got Gussie MacLellan into the promoting business and bankrolled some of his fights. MacDougall had fought for Gaum before. A big fight was coming up in Glace Bay that was to feature Blair Richardson in his first ten-round bout. Gaum needed someone to box on the under card. MacDougall's wife, however, would hear nothing of it.

According to MacDougall, Gaum returned two days later with a fistful of money, which he put on the table in front of MacDougall. MacDougall recalls, "Oh, you know, your eyes light up. When you're working for fifty bucks a week and you see a bunch of money on the table. So he said, 'That's yours Gordie if you'll sign for the fight'." MacDougall talked his wife into it, then asked Gaum when the fight was. Gaum told him the fight was in ten days. MacDougall spent the next ten days training, then hitchhiked to the fight because no one came to pick him up. He fought the other boxer to a draw.

Gordie MacDougall eventually left both the woods and boxing behind and started working on ships carrying coal, iron ore, grain and gypsum around the world. He visited ports in Europe, Africa, the Caribbean, the United States and South America. After twenty years of sailing he entered the Coast Guard. After five years in the Coast Guard Gordie developed Ameotrophic Lateral Sclerosis, otherwise known as Lou Gehrig's Disease, which is a terminal disease of the nervous system with no known cure or medication. Having recently lost his twenty-year-old son and having dealt with a chronic and near fatal drinking problem, and having survived numerous setbacks in boxing and in life in general, it seemed that Gordie MacDougall had been given his share of misery to endure without adding a fatal illness to the mix. But he was able to overcome even that, and managed to live with his ALS as best as one could.

In the early 1990s, Gordie recalled that he'd been all over the world, had met some great people and, after all those years and all those ups and downs, was happily married to his wife Shirley. His only sorrow was to see young people grow up and never see or do anything with their lives. "For them, I feel bad. But me, I've done everything and fulfilled my life." It was as if Gordie MacDougall felt deep in his soul that the point of life was to be anything but nothing. The point was to get out there and be someone— even if you get hurt along the way, no matter how tough it gets, no matter how low you go, it is still better than striving for nothing more than simply existing. Had those lights on the boxing ring shone just a bit brighter, had the spirits that haunt the darkness of the ring's periphery been angels and not wraiths, MacDougall is one of those Cape Breton fighters that might have gained entry to that realm of boxing nobility where he and all who knew him felt he truly belonged. But it didn't work out that way for the determined kid from South Bar with the wicked jab. Rudy Plichie notes that MacDougall could have gone all the way if he'd been given the chance to fight for a Canadian or even British Empire title.[7] That never happened for MacDougall though. But in many other ways, he did go all the way. Gordie MacDougall died in 1992 at the age of fifty-seven.

ROUND NINE:
THE ANGEL OF MERCY, RUDY PLICHIE

Someone had to stop the blood. It was everywhere. There was blood in the Glace Bay Miners Forum, the Venetian Gardens, the Sydney Forum and every other hockey rink, community hall and gymnasium where boxers met and did battle. The boxer can't stop the bleeding. When the blood flows into the eyes from a cut eyelid or eyebrow, it doesn't matter to the fighter. He wants only to keep fighting, bloodied or not. But it does matter to the referee, the judges and the ringside doctor. A bleeding boxer, as they say, is bad for business. So when a cut is open, it must be sealed. If not, your fighter will likely lose.

The trainer can't stop the flow of blood. He's there to pace his fighter. He's there to watch the other guy, too. He's busy looking for mistakes, shortcomings, weaknesses in the opponent that his fighter can exploit: something, anything, he can capitalize on. The trainer got you there, yes, but when you're in the ring and you're fighting for your life, when everything's on the line and you catch a punch that opens a bloody gash above your eye—someone has to stop the bleeding. You need a cut man. A guy with rolls of bandages, vials of coagulant and other potions, and years of expertise in knowing just what to do to stop the bleeding, close over a cut, and get you back into the ring—all in less than 60 seconds. A good cut man is part scientist, part doctor, and if he's really good, part magician. And while we're at it, part guardian angel, too. Entering the ring without one is dangerous and foolhardy; entering the ring with a good one can win you a fight. For many Cape Breton boxers, there was one man who was their guardian angel. There was one man who could stop the bleeding. Every time.

That man was Rudy Plichie.

Born in Glace Bay in 1934, Plichie started boxing at the age of fourteen and fought in twenty-nine amateur fights, winning all but one, which he fought to a draw. Plichie's brother, Johnny, was also active in boxing and promoted a number of fights at the Table Head Club in Glace Bay. Plichie recalls that their mother used to make their boxing trunks for them as well the tapes they used to wrap their hands with. There were a number of good boxers living in his neighbourhood, including Stevie "Kid" MacDonald, as well as the boxing promoter Gussie MacLellan. "With all these boxing personalities in the area, I just couldn't help but get involved," says Plichie in *Italian Lives, Cape Breton Memories.*[1]

Plichie didn't want to go professional as a boxer and instead turned to the world of training and managing. This eventually led him to lifelong service in the Cape Breton boxing fraternity as trainer and cut man. Plichie got his start in the "administration of boxing," as he calls it, with Johnny Cechetto at the Police Club at Sydney's Venetian Gardens. Plichie considered the Venetian Gardens one of the best boxing clubs around and a breeding ground for good fighters. In the twenty years Cechetto ran the gym, he and Plichie trained some of the great Cape Breton champions there, including Tyrone Gardiner, Rocky MacDougall and Ronnie Sampson. Sampson won the Canadian lightweight title from Willie Williams in 1966, shortly after Tyrone Gardiner retired undefeated with the same title, making him the fifth Cape Bretoner to hold a national title in the span of two years. Sampson was also the youngest boxer ever to win a boxing crown, doing so before his sixteenth birthday.

A large part of Plichie's early interest in developing boxers can be directly linked to the success of Johnny Cechetto. Upon hearing of Cechetto's retirement from training, Tony Unitas, founder of the Canadian Boxing Hall of Fame, wrote in 1978 that Cechetto was "one of the great boxing teachers the game had to offer. He is a man of great wisdom for the game of boxing and his retirement is a great loss to the boxing sport." According to Unitas, Cechetto personally paid for the upkeep of the sport he loved so well. Plichie himself saw boxing as a hobby and never took a cent for his work. He says that because the

Fig. 9.1. (Left to right) Ronnie Sampson, Rudy Plichie and Mike Bates. Photographer unknown. Courtesy Rudy Plichie.

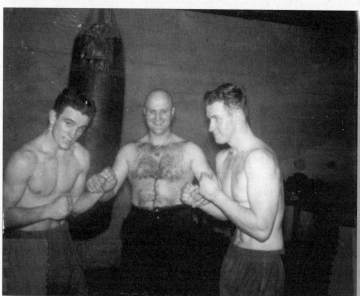

promoters knew him and his work so well they'd simply take him along and pick up the tab for him wherever they went.

Of all the people involved in getting a boxer ready for a bout and standing by him when he steps into the ring, the cut man is often the least noticed by the fans, though his role is often crucial. In Tyrone Gardiner's classic fight against Fern "The Bull" Chretien, it was the quick work of Rudy Plichie that helped win the fight.[2] Gardiner had suffered a major cut and without getting a speedy ringside repair job would have lost on a technical knockout. According to Plichie, "That was the toughest, bloodiest, scariest fight I ever worked."[3]

When a boxer gets cut in the ring it can spell catastrophe—not just for the fighter but for his entire entourage. Once the first blood starts to flow, it's the cut man who experiences the biggest adrenalin rush in the arena, as well as the biggest sense of dread. Once a fighter lands back on his stool, the cut man has about fifty seconds to stop the flow of blood. The cut may not be that serious, but since most cuts are over the eyes it's the dripping blood that causes the problem, sometimes obstructing the boxer's vision to the point of blindness. A fighter that can't see is going to get cut again. As every fighter knows, your opponent is going to aim at your cut. He'll want to reopen it. He'll want to get the blood flowing again so you can't see. It's a brutal and savage game that boxers play when it comes to bleeding; it's the way many fights are won or lost. As well, cuts around the eye can damage the tear ducts, and if the eyes go dry the fighter can't see. And that may be just one fight. There is also the ever present threat of permanent damage to a boxer's vision over the course of a long career.

Over the years, Rudy Plichie honed the skills and mastered the materials that control boxing induced bleeding. Prior to the start of a bout, Plichie would show the ringside physician what he had in his medical kit to make sure everything was approved for use. Plichie used a number of substances to control bleeding through their chemical activity. These included: adrenaline in a 1/1000 dilution; thromboplastin, either powdered or in a mixed solution; avetene, which is a collagen hemostat and a gel foam made of absorbable gelatin and thrombin mixed with saline; bismuth subgallate to treat facial lacerations; tincture of iodine to help stop nosebleeds.[4] Plichie also used a metal pressure plate to reduce swelling on the face. If the plate were applied to an injury properly, it would move accumulating fluid under the skin without destroying tissue. If a fighter's pulse was too fast (which increases blood flow) an ice bag placed over the heart would help slow the heart rate. To make a long story short, the general basis of action for the cut man is to apply the proper amounts and types of these various substances to specific injuries and then hope they'll force the blood vessels to draw together and stop the flow of blood. Don't forget that you're between rounds doing this, so you have less than a minute. And of course, sometimes you are expected to carry out these very exacting procedures under bad lighting conditions, surrounded by 5,000 screaming fans, and with a trainer barking orders into the ear of your dazed, bleeding patient. The cut game ain't easy. And it's certainly not for the faint of heart.

Any expert on boxing—and many boxers themselves—will tell you that the art of the game boils down to one single tenet: Don't get hit. For many boxers, avoiding punches is a more important part of their strategy than throwing them. Many world champions have embraced this philosophy, and to have a reputation of being "hard to hit" makes any fighter proud. And why not, as it speaks to grace, speed and technical precision. But even the best defensive fighter gets hit. It's inevitable. It's how you deal with it when it happens that can make all the difference. So for those times when a boxer finds himself on "Queer Street" (to boxing linguists, a boxer is said to be on Queer Street when he is all but out on his feet, dazed, seeing stars) and he manages to hang on for the bell and stagger back to his corner, it is his cut man that he needs most. Even the trainer will step aside to let the cut man work. And the cut man handles more than just cuts. When a fighter needs help to regain his senses, for example, cut men carry small pellets of ammonia (often referred to as ammonia bombs) to jolt a fighter back into reality. One sniff is usually enough to rouse even the most dazed of fighters. But while Plichie carried ammonia bombs, he preferred to use a sniff of vinegar instead, because ammonia increases blood pressure, which will cause increased bleeding if the fighter is also cut. Always thinking, was Plichie. Always thinking.

Plichie credits Al Bachman of New York with getting him seriously interesting in patching up fighters and becoming a successful cut man. According to Plichie, "Bachman had a special salve made by the famous boxing trainer Charlie Goldman. Right to this day I am the only Canadian that knows the recipe for that salve. I use it in the corner only with the permission of the doctor." (Charlie Goldman was legendary throughout boxing circles, and was best known as Rocky Marciano's trainer. Marciano, of course, was one of the greatest heavyweight champions of all time, and the only one to retire undefeated. Marciano hung up his gloves for good in 1955 with an astonishing record of 49-0.)

While cut men are required to reveal what ointments and potions they bring to the ring in their magic bag of healing tricks, they don't necessarily have to reveal the combinations and mixtures they concoct. This gives them a competitive edge over others. Plichie explains that the salve he acquired from Goldman's recipe for quick cessation of bleeding was "a combination of thrombin powder and adrenalin mixed with a certain amount of wax to keep it hard and soft. Then you use a combination of gel foam. This won't damage the tissue at all." There are countless other techniques Plichie employed depending on the extent of the injury to his fighter.

During his career in the corner of the ring, Plichie was cut man for more British Empire champions than anyone else in boxing. He was cut man for Gomeo Brennan in his two battles with the great Blair Richardson. Brennan was champ at the time of the first fight in which he retained his crown before losing it in the rematch with Richardson. Richardson retired a few months after winning the middleweight crown from Brennan, leaving the title vacant. Plichie recalls that the most memorable fight he was involved in—and played a crucial role in helping to win—was the match between Jamaica's Milo Calhoun and Jim Muellar of Windsor, Ontario, for the British Empire middleweight crown left vacant by Richardson. The fight was staged at the Glace Bay Miners Forum. The date was July 30, 1967. (As a point of interest, Calhoun's manager was none other than George Gainsford, best known for his years managing the great Sugar Ray Robinson, whom many regarded as the best pound-for-pound boxer the world had seen up to that time.) With the championship bout strategically planned for Glace Bay in order to maximize attendance, Gainsford needed a good cut man, preferably one from the local area. Al Bachman, who'd given Plichie his start, quickly convinced Gainsford that the man for the job was Rudy Plichie. Bachman himself was managing the opposing fighter, Jim Muellar, while Charlie Goldman was his trainer. That the great trainers like George Gainsford, Charlie Goldman and Cus D'Amato, whose protégés included the likes of Rocky Marciano, Sugar Ray Robinson and Mike Tyson, brought their fighters all the way to tiny Cape Breton Island lent credence to Cape Breton's having become known as the cradle of Canadian boxing. The legendary Jack Dempsey even visited Cape Breton to see and meet the local boxing talent. And even though the Calhoun-Muellar title bout did not feature a Cape Bretoner, it was because a Cape Breton fighter had previously held the title that the match was staged in Cape Breton rather than anywhere else in the entire British Empire.

Fig. 9.2. (Foreground left to right): Blair Richardson, trainer Johnny Nemis, Jack Dempsey and Gordie MacDougall. Gussie MacLellan in the background. 1960. Abbass Studios Collection, Beaton Institute, Cape Breton University, A-5931.

Cape Bretoners were in love with boxing at this time and everyone throughout the boxing world, especially promoters, knew it. Anyone involved in the fight game of the 1960s, anywhere in the world, knew of this small island off

Canada's rugged east coast that was not just a boxing hotbed, but that was itself producing an inordinate number of top rank fighters. So the Glace Bay Miners Forum hosted the British Empire Middleweight title bout because the Glace Bay Miners Forum was one of the best and most respected boxing venues in North America, and because the fights that were held there brought out in record numbers some of the sport's most passionate and knowledgeable fans. Rudy Plichie looked back on the Calhoun-Muellar bout—and the pivotal role he played in it:

Fig. 9.3. (Left to right): referee Bob Beaton, Milo Calhoun, Rudy Plichie and manager George Gainsford. British Empire middleweight championship. Calhoun (Jamaica) defeated Jim Mulleur of Windsor, ON, for title left vacant after Blair Richardson's retirement. Glace Bay Miners Forum. 1966. Clipping courtesy Tyrone Gardiner.

"Calhoun got a very nasty cut on the inside of his mouth, around the second round. I kept it closed ... and he won. That really stands out because you couldn't see the cut. It was one of the worst types of cuts you can handle in boxing because once you start swallowing your own blood it can be an awful handicap. We were very fortunate to stop that cut. It was four or five inches long, inside the mouth, and it went down through the jaw from the earlobe. That's one of the things you very rarely run into, but I had the right stuff to stop it. I used a powdered mixture of thromboplastin. This was the only way the cut could be stopped. That was really an exciting bout."

In the heat of the moment, with less than a minute between rounds to do his job, a cut man can't spend a lot of time puzzling over how a cut occurred. But after the Calhoun-Muellar fight, Plichie checked into things with the new champ, Milo Calhoun. Plichie learned that a month before the fight Calhoun had one of his back teeth filled. This caused his custom-made mouthpiece to be slightly offset. A couple of shots to the jaw and the ill-fitting mouth piece began to dig into Calhoun's mouth and cut him open. Without the capable skills and knowledge of Rudy Plichie that night, Milo Calhoun might have lost the British Empire crown because of a dental filling.

Another memorable fight for Plichie was in 1967 when he was working with Les Gillis, a New Waterford boxer who was fighting for the North American Junior Lightweight championship in New Glasgow. Gillis, who was already the Canadian champion, defeated Tibby Brown and became the first Canadian ever to win the North American crown for this weight class. One of the reasons the fight is memorable for Plichie is because Gillis, in Plichie's estimation, was the best "thinking fighter" he'd ever worked with.[5] "It was Gillis's ring craft, which always included extraordinary physical and mental conditioning, along with his being a southpaw with a hard-to-hit bob-and-weave style, that proved too much for Brown," said Plichie. "The feinting, slipping and counter-punching of Gillis completely fooled Brown time and again until he was counted out in the seventh round. Most fighters use their legs and arms for defence, but with Gillis it was all ring smarts." According to the cut man, Les Gillis was so smart in the ring, so deft on his feet and so good at avoiding punches, that he never sustained any serious cuts and left all of his ten- and twelve-round fights unmarked.

Fig. 9.4. Les Gillis, Canadian and North American junior lightweight champion, 1966, 1967. Photographer unknown. Courtesy Rudy Plichie.

Les Gillis became the fifth Cape Bretoner in the mid 1960s, following Gardiner, Richardson, MacDougall and Sampson, to win a national—and in his case, international—championship. Plichie had Gillis signed up to fight for the World Junior Lightweight title against Flash Elorde of the Philippines. Now enshrined in the International Boxing Hall of Fame, Elorde, who retired in 1971 with an 88-27-2 record, is described by the IBHOF as "one of the greatest fighters to ever come out of the Asia-Pacific region." Unfortunately for Gillis, the fight never came off because Elorde's team didn't want their man, a southpaw, to fight another southpaw.

This is another example of the cruel whims of the seemingly uncaring boxing gods, and whether or not they choose to smile on you. Had Gillis been given the opportunity to fight Elorde, an opportunity he had earned and deserved, and had he won, his career and life might have turned out quite differently. But because of a decision by Elorde's management team to not fight a southpaw at this stage of their fighter's career, Gillis was denied a momentous opportunity. More poignantly, there was nothing Gillis could do about it. No matter how hard he worked, no matter how good he got, no matter how many fights he won, the decision was the champion's to make and the champion decided that he did not want to fight Les Gillis. But that's boxing, where conditions and dynamics beyond your control whirl around you constantly. Sometimes, the planets align and you find yourself fighting for a title; sometimes, they don't, and no matter how good you are—and you may even be better than the fighter who *does* get the title shot—it doesn't

Fig. 9.5. Les Gillis vs. Buddy Daye for Canadian Junior Lightweight championship. Savoy Theatre, Glace Bay. 1966. Abbass Studios Collection, Beaton Institute, Cape Breton University, B-4689c.

Fig. 9.6. Gomeo Brennan, Izzy Klein and promoter Gussie MacLellan looking through *Ring Magazine*, before second title match against Blair Richardson for British Empire middleweight championship. March 1966. Abass Photographic Studio, Beaton Institute B-5029.

matter: You don't get your shot and that's that. End of story.

Despite the twist of fate that befell him, Les Gillis nevertheless left the fight game with an esteemed reputation, not to mention a solid record of 28-5 over a ten-year career, retiring as Canadian Super Featherweight champion. Tony Unitas, president of the Canadian Boxing Hall of Fame, rightly summed up the career of Les Gillis as "Distinction earned, recognition deserved."

From Gillis to Calhoun and all points in between, according to Plichie, he's never had a fight stopped because he couldn't repair a cut. If a fighter could last the round with an injury and make it back to his stool at the end of the round, than Rudy was able to get him fixed. Plichie believes one of the worst things that could happen in the ring is to have a referee call a fight before the cut man has had a chance to repair his fighter.

Fans also play a part in any boxing match and can even have a negative effect on their own fighter if the cut man loses his edge. With all the screaming and yelling going on, it isn't easy to think clearly and work fast. Plichie says, "You can't be intimidated by the crowd and the noise, because you could end up harming the boxer if you are not aware and careful." Plichie describes what its like to work as a cut man in a major bout:

"You have to work fast. You only have fifty seconds to work with. The clock starts ticking as soon as the bell rings to end the round and the boxer may take up to four or five seconds just getting to the corner. You have to be ready. You can't spend several valuable seconds unscrewing bottles and opening cases. You have to recognize the problem, know how to work around it, and maintain your composure."

Plichie goes on to emphasize the importance of working quickly yet not appearing to hurry, or seem anxious. The boxer can sense the urgency of the situation and unless the cut man can reassure him by fixing his wounds it may affect the boxer's performance in the next round. "And the other team may gain confidence," says Plichie, "if they think it's a serious cut."

His skill as a cut man and his role as a boxing trainer and conditioner became so well known within the international boxing community that he was asked to serve on the International Ratings Panel for *Ring Magazine*, long considered boxing's bible. Plichie was the first Canadian to serve on this prestigious panel. He believes he was the first Canadian to be inducted into the Canadian boxing hall of fame as a cut man. Over the span of his career, the Cape Bretoner worked with five Canadian Champions.

Plichie's career as a cut man and boxing conditioner extended well into the 1980s and 1990s due to his expertise and his incredible success with keeping boxers in the match. He worked with New Waterford's Roddie MacDonald, the "Tartan Terror," in his fight for the vacant world cruiserweight title held in 1983 in Halifax, a bout which MacDonald ultimately lost to the American Marvin Camel by a TKO in the fifth.

Fig. 9.7. Roddie MacDonald, "Tartan Terror of New Waterford." 1986. Photographer unknown. Courtesy Rudy Plichie.

Fig. 9.8. Rudy Plichie repairing cuts to Roddie MacDonald during World cruiserweight title match vs. Mervin Camel (Dec. 1983). Clipping (Jan. 18, 1984) courtesy Rudy Plichie.

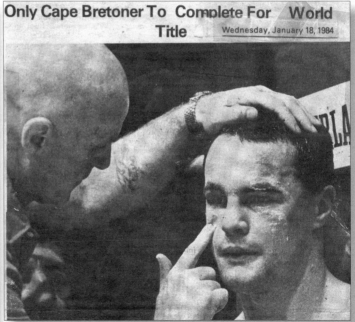

Only Cape Bretoner To Complete For World Title Wednesday, January 18, 1984

In 1992, Plichie was credited with a major role in Gerry Meekison's victory over Mohammad Eltassi at the Halifax Forum. Meekison was a known bleeder, prone to cuts over the eye and his trainer wanted the best in the business because he anticipated the fight was going to be a "bloody mess." According to Plichie, Meekison suffered a number of cuts that "were wide but not deep." Plichie was called on twice to repair the bleeding Meekison who, while bloody, was fighting a good fight. Plichie was able to keep Meekison in the fight until the end and Meekison was awarded the decision and the Eastern Canadian Middleweight crown. *Daily News* sports writer Pat Connolly wrote after the fight, "Colonel Plichie's herbs and spices (his cut substances and techniques) have breathed new life into Gerry Meekison's boxing future and perhaps into the immediate well-being of the game in these parts."[6]

Rudy Plichie played a key role in keeping the fight game going in Cape Breton through a combination of heart and mind. The trainers, managers, promoters, boxers and fight fans of Cape Breton were one huge family in the years following the Second World War and on up through to the late 1960s. But by the time the Tyrone Gardiners, Blair Richardsons, Rocky MacDougalls, Ronnie Sampsons and Les Gillis' were through, so were many other great local boxing heroes. Add to this the fact that trainers of the status of the two Johnnies—Nemis and Cechetto—were no longer around, and promoter extraordinaire Gussie MacLellan was getting older and proving irreplaceable. Even Rudy Plichie's medicine and magic couldn't stop the bleeding that would come when the Cape Breton fight scene received its fateful, and fatal, knockout punch.

ROUND TEN:
TECHNICAL KNOCKOUT

During the late 1960s, Cape Breton's boxing culture had begun to show signs that it might be weakening. That things were beginning to unravel was due to combination of factors and could not be attributed to any one single blow. Indeed, as early as 1963 Earle Pemberton had written in his boxing bulletin *Punching with Pemberton* that things were starting to suffer in the local boxing scene.

"Today we have no good amateur boxers in Cape Breton. In fact, after Blair Richardson, Tyrone Gardiner and Rocky MacDougall are finished we have nothing. Unless small clubs are established and young talent developed it looks as if we will be running out of local performers."

Two years after Earle Pemberton wrote these words, all three boxers he had mentioned were Canadian Champions. By 1966 Les Gillis and Ronnie Sampson had also joined their ranks as National Champions. While 1965 and 1966 were glorious years for the Cape Breton boxing community, the words of the boxing scribe were ominous. In that same 1963 article, Pemberton wrote, "I believe Sydney shoemaker Johnny Cechetto is the only person in Cape Breton who has honestly and sincerely tried to keep to keep the

Fig. 10.1.
Ronnie Sampson,
Canadian lightweight
champion. 1966.
Photographer unknown.
Courtesy Rudy Plichie.

small boxing clubs going." MacDougall, Gardiner and Richardson were all affiliated one way or another with Cechetto at the time of their combined triple crown in 1965.

If one looks hard enough and connects the dots, reasons for the decline of boxing in Cape Breton emerge. In 1964, for example, the venerable Venetian Gardens, hallowed ground to the Cape Breton boxing community, was destroyed by fire, though it was rebuilt. Also in 1964, the Canadian Armed Forces cancelled its boxing program, the same year that serviceman—and Cape Bretoner—Eddie MacKillop was one of Canada's top prospects for a medal at the Olympic Games in Tokyo. Johnny Nemis, the man who was part of the initial impetus in the surge of great Cape Breton boxers in the 1960s, began his career as a boxing trainer in the Canadian Military. This decision must have been discouraging to Nemis and others who got their start in boxing in the army. And by the late 1960s, Nemis was just about through with the fight game. The tragic 1960 death of Nemis's last hope for a champion, the young and prodigiously gifted Ernie MacKinnon of South Bar, had already done much to pull the mat out from under the trainer. In many ways, the end of the military boxing program and the destruction by fire of the Venetian Gardens notwithstanding, many would point to the death of Ernie MacKinnon as the first nail in the coffin of the Cape Breton boxing fraternity.

And as Johnny Nemis's role in boxing began to wane, so did that of the other Johnny, Johnny Cechetto. Johnny Cechetto had run a successful shoe repair shop in Sydney for over 50 years and spent most of his spare time involved with boxing. Time and again, boxers have emphasized that Cechetto did it all for the love of the sport and was never financially involved. By the late 1960s, however, with an ever-decreasing number of boxers coming up through the local system, and due to increasing ill health and a desire to spend more time with his family, Cechetto considerably scaled back his role in boxing. [1]

Fig. 10.2. Venetian Gardens in flames. 1964. Photographer unknown. Courtesy Gordon McVicar.

Then, in 1971, Cape Breton fight fans learned that their golden haired hero, Blair Richardson, former British Empire Middleweight champion, had died in Boston. Halifax city planner and Sydney native Kemp MacDonald was twelve years old at the time and remembers when he was told about Richardson's death at elementary school hockey.

"I was in grade six at Argyle School and our coach was Charlie Long. He came into the dressing room and told us Blair Richardson had passed away that day. It was like we had a major hero die. Even though I hadn't seen any of his fights, I knew Blair Richardson's death was a big deal at the time for older people."[2]

Though Richardson had been out of the fight game for several years when he had died, many fans felt that his tragic, early death was yet another harbinger of the bad times ahead for Cape Breton boxing.

Though managers and trainers continued to try and get younger men involved in boxing, there weren't many left with the drive and commitment of the two Johnnies. Those who managed to keep the sport breathing after Nemis and Cechetto included Tom Gordon from the Northside and Jimmie MacInnis and Henry Rideout of Glace Bay. Rideout was well known for teaching his fighters the science of boxing, and according to Rudy Plichie, Rideout taught his fighters what he called the "lost art of blocking, guarding and feinting" in boxing.[3] Rideout, MacInnis and Gordon were all inducted into the Canadian Boxing Hall of Fame as boxing builders in 1987 for their role in trying to keep the boys punching in Cape Breton.

As fight fans and fighters look back on the heyday of Cape Breton boxing, no other name comes up as often as that of Gussie MacLellan. MacLellan was a promoter of extraordinary talent who was as well connected to the international boxing scene as anyone could be. World renowned boxing promoter Al Bachman of New York once told Rudy Plichie, "Gussie was

Fig. 10.3. Ronnie Sampson training with John Cechetto. 1966. Abbass Studios Collection, Beaton Institute, Cape Breton University, B-5831.

Fig. 10.4. Trio of Champs: Blair Richardson, Tyrone Gardiner, Rocky MacDougall. 1965. Abbass Studios Collection, Beaton Institute, Cape Breton University, B-4450b.

as good as any boxing promoter in the world."[4] Unfortunately, with fewer local fighters to draw from, MacLellan's stable of talent began to decline. And as he aged it became obvious that no one could take his place. Without someone of MacLellan's caliber to work the backrooms of the money men and the gyms of the fighters with equal skill and passion, it appeared that Cape Breton's relationship with the fight game was coming to an end.

When asked about the decline of boxing in Cape Breton in the 1970s, veteran boxer Allie Steele remarked, "Well, when Johnny Nemis died in 1974, and Gussie MacLellan became ill and was out of the picture, there really wasn't anybody to glue the whole together. And I'd probably say the end of the era around here would be the demise of Blair Richardson. You know at that time, professional boxing, for all intents and purposes, was just about finished."[5]

Steele emphasized the role Gussie MacLellan played in keeping boxing alive and how the vacuum created after he left the game simple couldn't be filled. According to Steele, "You've got to have a promoter that was prepared to put the money in to make the thing go. Gussie was the man that did that, because it took money to bring these fighters in and keep these contacts going, and Gussie wasn't afraid to put the money into promotion to get it. He had the contacts, he knew the fighters, he had all the information he needed, and he put together some pretty successful cards." Former broadcaster and media sports director Dave LeBlanc described MacLellan as a thorough boxing promoter who always treated his

Fig. 10.5. Gussie MacLellan (left) and Jack Dempsey (right), with unidentified man. Photographer unknown. Courtesy Tyrone Gardiner.

fighters well. "Gussie put up his money and was willing to take the risk," said LeBlanc.[6] Former Canadian Featherweight Champion and Olympic boxing referee Rocky MacDougall fondly recalls MacLellan as a smooth-talking businessman who knew the world of boxing game and promotion. "He was a fighter going back into the 1930s and 1940s. He was an old time promoter, smiling all the time. He was nice and he had a very soft voice, and he always managed to show you why you should fight for him. Gussie was a unique character who came along in the 1930s and 1940s. If you look at the old movies you see these old boxing promoters and that's the way he was."

Rudy Plichie recalls that MacLellan had a way with people he's never seen with anyone else. In one memorable moment in Halifax while negotiating an upcoming fight, MacLellan remarked to a Halifax promoter that he liked his three-piece suit, and then quickly added, "Did you buy it new?" Many former fighters and fans agree that if Gussie MacLellan wasn't on the Cape Breton fight scene in the 1940s onward, Cape Breton's incredible boxing success may never have happened. An unmarried man all his life, Gussie MacLellan played matchmaker for boxers and their loyal fans for forty years. MacLellan continued to promote fights well into the 1970s, though they were less frequent than in the post-war years. In one of his last contests, staged in Halifax at the Metro Centre in 1979, a record crowd of over 10,000 showed up to see former Montreal Olympic boxer and Halifax native Chris Clarke take on and beat Toronto slugger Clyde Grey for the British Empire welterweight title.[7] In a MacLellan promoted rematch held in Halifax three months later the tables were turned and Grey took the title back from the champion Clarke. Grey fought for the World welterweight belt three times over his career but was never able to win the coveted prize.

Fig. 10.6. Willie Williams and two unidentified young fighters with trainer John Cechetto and promoter Gussie MacLellan. 1958. Abbass Studios Collection, Beaton Institute, Cape Breton University, A-2972.

Over the years, many people had asked MacLellan who he thought was the best Cape Breton boxer. Smooth as ever, MacLellan always sidetracked the question to avoid playing favorites, but once later on in years he did admit that the fighter who was without a doubt the biggest draw was George Ross. For MacLellan, Ross had "It," which in the boxing world was something that didn't come easily or frequently.

Rudy Plichie described Gussie MacLellan as an incredibly generous person who often made sure people in need didn't go hungry or without the essentials. Long before we had maternity leaves, Plichie remembers MacLellan telling a waitress who was pregnant that she couldn't wait tables in the bar he ran until her baby was born. However, he continued to pay her. This side of Gussie wasn't known to a lot of people who recognized him mainly as a promoter. "Gussie often told me he never sold a ticket in his life, either," said Plichie. "Gussie would say if you promoted the fight right, treated everyone fair and made the fans happy, then they'd come and buy a ticket." Once Gussie was gone, that was it, said Plichie. "We'll never see a guy like him again."

Radio played an important role in boxing's heyday because it brought the fights to those fans who couldn't get to the packed venues. Dave LeBlanc

Fig. 10.7. (Left to right): cutman Rudy Plichie, Lonnie States vs. Ronnie Sampson and Tyrone Gardiner as referee. 1966. Abbass Studios Collection, Beaton Institute, Cape Breton University, B-4708.

Fig. 10.8. (Left to right): cutman Rudy Plichie, trainer John Cechetto, Rocky MacDougall and Eric Cechetto. Raytel photo courtesy Ray Doucette.

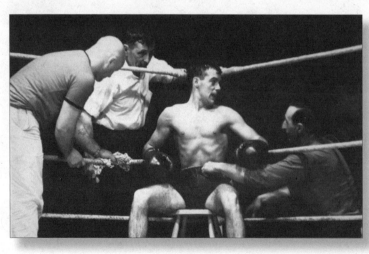

credits longtime radio broadcaster Donnie MacIsaac with being a big part of promoting boxing before the advent of television. "Television started here in 1955, so many people still didn't have it in the 1960s. Donnie did a great job on CJCB and Aubrey Keizer did a lot with his columns in the *Cape Breton Post*. Ace Foley wrote good columns for the *Chronicle Herald,* too. Russ Doyle covered a lot of the fights also," said LeBlanc. According to Dave LeBlanc the eventual decline in print and radio journalism over the years seemed to coincide with the demise of Cape Breton boxing as well.

Local photographers also played a major role in promoting fights of the day. The Abbass brothers took numerous visually stunning photos for the *Cape Breton Post* and Ray Doucette, who went by the moniker Raytel, recorded many ring battles with his experienced eye for the *Cape Breton Highlander.* "I used to be right in the corner. There'd be up to four of us, one in each corner taking pictures," said Doucette in a 2009 conversation. "It was nothing to get sprayed with blood and sweat during a fight. Nobody worried about the things we worry about today back then."[8] Unbeknownst to the great Cape Breton photographers of the day they were documenting the slow progressive decline of a great period in local sporting history.

As Cape Breton boxing began its slide in the early 1970s to become a more obscure sport practised only by the few, the role of cable television and the celebrity aspect of world heavyweight championships began to replace the glory days of crowded forums and dance halls throughout Cape Breton and the Maritimes in general.

With less fights to go to, it became easier for people to simply stay at home and get involved with the latest TV programming. Friday night fights were replaced by shows like *Dallas,* and the athleticism and wholesomeness of professional boxing, Cape Breton style, was replaced by the cash driven glitz-and-glam spectacle that the world boxing scene was fast in the process of becoming. And while money had never played much of a role in the lives of Cape Breton boxers during the Golden Age from the 1940s through to the late 1960s (in those days, they truly were in it for the love of the sport), by the 1980s money had come to rule practically all sports, including boxing. Promoters staged fights at Centre 200 in Sydney but according to Allie Steele, the outlay was too much. "They were paying these guys way too much money," said Steele. "We knew it wasn't going to work because there wasn't a good local fighter. The way Gussie and Johnny Nemis did it, they developed the local fighters on the local scene. There were enough fighters here locally; you didn't have to bring anybody. New Waterford, Glace Bay, Sydney, they put on barn burners. The old *Cape Breton Post* gave good write-ups to the fighters, it really played up well, people were interested and they all had their favorites who'd become main-eventers."

By the 1990s, however, it would be hard to find a single person walking the streets of Glace Bay, Sydney, North Sydney or New Waterford that could name a single boxer that was training in their home town. Though some small gyms survived, most people wouldn't even be able to tell you where they were. If you asked anyone when the next night of fights would be taking place, you'd get nothing but a funny look in return. The distinction so rightly earned by the early Cape Breton boxers and deservedly recognized by their legion of fans was beginning to vanish. For all intents and purposes, Cape Breton boxing had sustained a series of blows and cuts from which it would not recover—and the entire community would be affected. That sense of fraternity, of being part of the crowd that enjoyed a real night out, was now over.

RE MATCH:
HOLY REDEEMER HALL, WHITNEY PIER 2006

We return to Whitney Pier....

It was more than eighty years ago that Joe Uvanni of New York took an interest in a young man from New Waterford by the name of Johnny Nemis and started teaching him the fundamentals of boxing at a makeshift gym set up in a warehouse in Whitney Pier. The Pier was forged of the molten metal of the Sydney Steel Plant and attracted people from around the world, of all nationalities and denominations, from 1900 through to the 1930s. Europeans and West Indians, especially, came in large numbers to settle and find new lives in a new, post-First World War environment. To satisfy the religious needs of so diverse a group of people, various churches were established.

At the time of this writing, Whitney Pier still hosts a Polish church, a Ukrainian church, an African Orthodox church, an Italian church and several others, including a museum that once was a Jewish Synagogue (members of the Jewish faith now attend a synagogue in Sydney). Holy Redeemer Church, at the far end of Victoria Road leading into South Bar, home to numerous famous boxers including Blair Richardson, is a majestic Church built in 1901 that takes care of the needs of the Pier's Catholic population. The church hall, situated behind the church, has been, over the decades, host to countless weddings, parties and anniversaries. Literally everyone in Industrial Cape Breton has visited Holy Redeemer Hall for one event or another. Even on this evening, there's dancing going on in Holy Redeemer Hall. But it's not the kind of dancing we see at weddings. It's the kind of dancing that takes place within the four corners of a boxing ring, a boxing ring set up in the center of the hall. The dancers on tonight's card, jogging lightly on the spot in the blue and red corners of the ring, represent some of the best amateur boxing hopefuls Cape Breton has to offer. They come from the Rhy-Mac boxing club in Sydney's North End district; the Tommy Gordon club from the Northside; Ring 73 in Glace Bay; and Dalton's Gym in the Pier. Mainland boxers are here as well, coming from Westville and Halifax, and there are also a couple of fighters who've made the trek from New Brunswick.

The idea to take boxing out of the training gyms and bring it back to the church halls for the fans to enjoy came from Dwayne Dalton, of Dalton's Gym. In 2005, the idea of staging a night of boxing in Whitney Pier took hold. Since then, at least half a dozen boxing matches featuring the best in local talent in their teens and early twenties have been held in the Pier. Once the boxing events began to catch on, it wasn't long before these evenings of boxing became sold out affairs. Children, girlfriends, parents, brothers and sisters all come out for fight night. Kids are roaming throughout the hall looking for the boxers of yesteryear, who are almost always in attendance, to sign their photocopied programs. Tyrone Gardiner, Gramps Kiley, Hilton Smith and Rudy Plichie are often there. In fact, Gardiner and Plichie, ever dedicated, ever helpful, can be spotted throughout Industrial Cape Breton putting up posters to help advertise the fights. Gardiner is so enthusiastic about the revival of boxing in Cape Breton that he thinks we'll be raising a champion within the next few years.

Not to let a good thing pass, Casino Nova Scotia has also been bringing in fighters, often from the United States military boxing programs, to tackle our local fight talent. The venue is located in downtown Sydney. The events are usually sold out long in advance of the night of the fight.

In December 2006, the Rhy-Mac club of Sydney hosted Friday Night Fights at the Holy Redeemer Hall. The main event was between middleweights Michael Gerrow of the Rhy-Mac club and Malcolm MacDonald from the Tommy Gordon club. From the shouts of the crowd of around 300 it was obvious both boxers had lots of hometown support. Sitting across and just behind my seven-year-old son, Samuel, and me was Gordon "Gramps" Kiley. Stoic as ever, Kiley watched the fight without so much as blinking. Observing Kiley, who represents an era gone by, I wondered what he was thinking. Was this the rebirth of a sporting era he and so many other young men of his day were lucky to be a part of? Perhaps.

Fig. 11.1. Holy Redeemer fight night. Courtesy Paul MacDougall.

FUTURE CARDS 2010

In a small non-descript building in the North End of Sydney resides the Sydney Boxing Club. Former boxer, trainer, promoter, husband and dad Brad Ross took over the club a few years ago changing the name from Rhy-Mac to the Sydney Boxing club.[1] Like Tyrone Gardiner before him Ross works at the Sydney Correctional Center and spends the rest of his time training young boxers and staging events at the Sydney Casino. Holy Redeemer Hall is now a mosque and Dalton's Gym has closed, but the kids are still interested and Ross has the enthusiasm needed for the job. In many ways he epitomizes the trainers and promoters who came before him. For Ross, it's all about the sport and setting kids on a good clean life path.

The club has a ring in the center and various punching bags hanging throughout. Photographs of old time boxers are stuck to the walls. There's a change room downstairs in the basement. Young guys are taping their hands and lacing up gloves. There's a feeling of excitement in the place. Ross leads the crew of a dozen or so fighters through a rigorous exercise regime then arranges sparring events for the next crop of local boxers. His wife Debbie is often at his side lacing gloves and helping out in various capacities. She's as much part of the Sydney Boxing Club as he is. Even his twelve-year-old daughter Taylor is into it and is training for her first match in between going to dance classes. Ross is organizing an upcoming match at Casino Nova Scotia in a couple of weeks. Tables of ten go for $200. "We're hoping for another sellout," he says. A lot of the tickets go simply by word of mouth. Gussie MacLellan would be proud.

Fig. 12.1. Melvin Skeete (left) and Neil Reid work out at the Sydney Boxing Club. Photo by Paul MacDougall.

Fig. 12.2. Boxing card at Membertou Trade and Convention Centre. 2010. Photo by Paul MacDougall.

Fig. 12.3. (left to right) Ryan MacPhee, Glenn Williams (Ass't Coach), Taylor Ross, Brad Ross (Coach), Neil Reid, Chad Burns (Ass't Coach) at Sydney Boxing Club. Photo by Paul MacDougall.

WHY A BOOK ABOUT CAPE BRETON BOXING?
AN AFTERWORD BY DAN MACDONALD, PHD

Why write a book about boxing? In 2006, a writer for *Sports Illustrated* claimed that ultimate fighting had overtaken boxing in terms of popularity.[1] Certainly the esteem of current UFC welterweight champion George St. Pierre from Quebec has enhanced the image of ultimate fighting here in Canada. Also, boxing is injurious. Recently there have been many stories in the news about the link between head trauma and dementia. One source suggests that head injury is the third most common cause of dementia in people younger than fifty years.[2] Varda Burstyn has suggested that because of its violence, boxing teaches us about the rewards of violence and hence about "coercive entitlement."[3] Of course this is nothing new for the sport as anti-boxing crusades have come and gone in history. If we contextualize boxing as a sport with a life-span of many centuries we see that it has been consistently up and down in terms of popularity. Often boxing has had the most unlikely of allies which have worked to legitimize it throughout its history.

The term boxing has its roots in Old English from about 600 years ago. It was meant to symbolize "fighting with fists,"[4] though it is unclear what the term "fight" actually meant. It was likely an impromptu method of settling disagreements through fists. In northern North America during the 1700s, boxing was much less formalized than what we see today. At trading posts, French Canadian and Metis voyageurs often engaged in contests of strength, brawling, drinking and fisticuffs. These masculine contests developed around a tavern culture in which fist-fighting and gambling on fights provided an important source of leisure and excitement for bachelors during traditional holidays at these trading posts.[5]

By the 19th century both Canada and the United States had developed a similar tavern culture. Boxing helped increase the sale of liquor and established bar keepers as important leaders of working class culture. From about the 1840s prizefighters found it in their best interest to make taverns their headquarters. Some fighters made enough money to own their own saloons while others managed and some simply visited frequently. Having notable prizefighters associated with particular taverns was good for the sale of liquor. Of course middle-class audiences abhorred the unholy trinity of naked brutality, drinking and rowdy working class patrons, that was associated with prizefighting. But from this boxers came to symbolize working class assertiveness and the successful flaunting of oppressive socio-cultural mores.

Across Canada boxing underwent a bourgeois assault, the result splitting the sport into two separate entities. Prizefighting was outlawed in the late 1800s for its apparent viciousness. Amateur boxing or sparring was given legitimization though by Cambridge University student, John Graham Chambers, who devised rules for the sport. The guide was published in 1867 by scholar Sir John Sholto Douglas, the eighth Marquis of Queensbury.

Many of the original rules are still in existence. Included was the introduction of standardized gloves, a limited number of three minute rounds, weight classifications, a consistent system of judging and refereeing, and disallowing wrestling. The new Queensbury Rules added much needed respect to the sport. Amateur boxing flourished in this new climate of respectability while bare knuckle prizefighting appeared to be slowly dying off.[6] The new comprehensive rules went far to sanitize the image of professional boxing and further distance it from the bare knuckle era.[7]

By the end of the 19th century, mainstream Protestant denominations espoused "muscular Christianity" which presented "an image of Christ as robust and manly."[8] Boxing was considered to offer important socialization for youths into manly ideals." Public attitudes toward the sport of boxing were gradually gaining acceptance. Along with moral endorsement, boxing clubs gained a further endorsement from the world of science. Under the proper conditions even a prize fight could be a scientific demonstration of technique, physicality and discipline. New techniques were considered scientific breakthroughs. Boxing was socially rationalized in a society becoming obsessed with "technique and rules."[9]

The image of boxing, especially amateur boxing, was recast as a modern and morally upright form of self discipline, but professional boxing still had its detractors. The sport could simply not evade accusations of brutality and persistent gambling. Anti-boxing crusaders continued their campaign. In many parts of Canada at the turn of the 20th century, professional boxing remained illegal.[10]

As the 20th century began, professional boxing became less of an oppositional way of living. It acted as a break from the rigours of modern everyday life. Though becoming mainstream, boxing hadn't yet become completely accepted. With the outbreak of the First World War boxing received further validation as a means of physical training and hand to hand combat for Canadian and American soldiers. Jeffrey Sammons has argued: "Indeed the barbarism of the real war made boxing seem dignified, if not dainty."[11] Even after the war-weariness experienced by the Canadian public, boxing reached a new stage of legitimacy and became primed for continued commercial development and exploitation. By the 1920s, Cape Breton was set to become a grand place for boxing. Young fighters from around local communities competed with one another for various titles, recognition and remuneration. This is the where this book began.

So why write a book about boxing when the sport features violence, trauma and coercive entitlement? The reason is that boxing often served as a cultural metaphor for life in Cape Breton communities. There were dozens of workers' strikes, corporate and state violence, the slow trauma of poverty and more than a little coercive entitlement by local employers. In fact, labour poet Dawn Fraser made a persuasive case for boxing as a cultural metaphor in his song/poem "Give Us a Fighting Man." In it Fraser, who often filled in as a timer for local boxing matches giving him the literary pseudonym of "Ole Timer," constructs a heroic Cape Breton boxer who is "rough and tough and clean, but never yellow, sore or mean." He is a working class warrior who is honourable and overtly masculine, who is charged with saving the industrial communities of Cape Breton. The last stanza reads:

> For old Cape Breton has had her fighting
> In many a bloody ring
> She fought Kid Strike and Kid Hard-Times,
> And old Kid Everything.
> It's not her style to stand and brag
> Over the titles she got.
> She's taken some awful lickings. Yes!
> But damn it she always fought.
> And when her next big battle comes,
> She'll do the best she can.
> And she'll welcome you, kid, and use you right.
> If you're a fighting man.[12]

Yes, boxing today is facing serious challenges. While it is not likely the sport will ever escape the seriousness of its participants undergoing head trauma, it will probably undergo a shift in training which increasingly emphasizes protection and safety of its fighters. As for ultimate fighting, well, I think it saved the sport of boxing. It did not help the commercial side of the sport which has always been susceptible to corruption, but it now functions as a legitimate portion of the training regime for ultimate fighters. Knowledge of wrestling, submission wrestling, kickboxing and mixed martial arts as well as boxing techniques make up today's successful ultimate fighters.

A return to the glory days of boxing in the 20th century may not be possible, which is why a history of the sport and recognition of the distinction earned by many local participants is so necessary and deserved, and answers the question "Why write a book about boxing?"

BOXING POEMS

The following poem has been adopted into Cape Breton boxing circles over the years. It was handed out by young boxers in 2006 before a card held at Holy Redeemer Hall in Whitney Pier. It was written by Vincent Caprani of Dublin, Ireland and published in a collection of his in 1982 which is now out of print. No one seems to know who first started using it at the Cape Breton fights but it's a fitting and appropriate way to start a boxing match and include in a book dedicated to the boxers of Cape Breton who could deliver a knockout punch.

"The Prizefighter's Prayer" by Vincent Caprani

I ask you not for victory, for somehow, that seems wrong.
But only for protection, and the courage to be strong.

Strength –not to conquer- but just that I'll fight well,
And prove myself a sportsman at the final bell.

I ask you Christ of Suffering, that should I suffer pain,
I'll offer it for all my sins so that it won't be in vain.

And if, perhaps, he cuts me, and the bright red blood I see,
I ask that I'll remember the blood you shed for me.

I need you in my corner, but likewise in the other,
So that I'll remember my opponent is my brother.

And I'll pray that you'll protect us from injuries severe,
That we'll give fans their value and every cause to cheer.

And make each single act of either one be fair,
So no matter who the victor, in the glory both can share.

And if, by chance, he floors me and the canvas I should meet,
Like Simon of Cyrene, please help me with my feet.

Then should a little glory somehow fall on me,
Please help me to remember that I owe it all to thee.

Please help me go the distance through rounds with danger rife,
Not only in the boxing square, but in the larger ring of life.

So I ask You not for Victory… for somehow that seems wrong,
But only for protection and the courage to be strong.

Strength of mind and body so I'll fight each battle well,
And the referee will raise my hand, at the Judgment's Final Bell.

...

A Tribute to Louis (Louie) Nemis

This poem was written by Earle Pemberton following Louie Nemis's death on February 15 1961. Though written especially for Louie Nemis, Earle's words are a fitting epithet for any and all boxers who have fought the good fight and made it to the final clanging of the bell.

This is a tribute to a boxer,
A knight of the resin trail;
Who made a good showing
In a game that's rough going
For a purse that's known as kale.

Yes, this is a tribute to a boxer,
Who thanked the good lord above,
For the strength to keep going,
And watch the game growing,
For his was a labor of love.

And here's to that boxer who left us
After giving many a thrill;
His ring-work is finished
But with pride undiminished
From Heaven he shines on us still.

WHO'S WHO

Herewith, some of the boxers active on the Cape Breton fight scene from the 1940s to the 1970s. Compiled with the help of Rudy Plichie, Tyrone Gardiner and Eddie McKillop. My apologies for missing anyone. I'm sure I've missed a few.

1940S AND 1950S

JB Kid Adshade
Kid Atkins
Berth Boone
Ernie Burchell
Johnny Cechetto - trainer
Artie Dalton
Benny DeLorenzo
Pat Fortune
Archie "Bear" Hannigan
Greg Hannigan
Al Hogan
Bobby Jackson
Mutt Kavluck
Gordon "Gramps" Kiley
Mitch Krszwada
Bill Laffin
Bobby Laffin
Nick Laffin
Ko MacKay
Gussie MacLellan - promoter
Mickey MacMullin

Paddy MacNeil
Ronnie MacNeil
Dempsey MacPhail
Red MacPherson
Nick Melnick
Mello Nearing
Joe Nemis
Johnny Nemis – trainer
Tony Odo
Bobby Pickles
Charlie Pyle
Joe Pyle
Billy Rideout
Henry Rideout
George "Rockabye" Ross
Lenny Ryan
Bucky Sampson
Tommy "Gun" Spencer
Geno Smith
Pordena Smith

1960s and 1970s

Bee Arsenault
Bobo Bonaparte
Bobby Curtis
Bobby Dalton
Johnny Devison
Johnny Fowler
Kevin Gallivan
Tyrone Gardiner
Boom Boom Gillis
Les Gillis
Billy Holm
Gordie MacDougall
Rocky MacDougall
Lambert MacIntosh

Charlie MacIntyre
Ernie MacKinnon
Lonnie MacNeil
Oats MacNeil
Joe MacPhee
Eddie McKillop
Bobby Moore
Kelly Oickle
Benny Red Randall
Blair Richardson
Clayton Ryan
Ronnie Sampson
Lawrence Spencer
Willie Williams

DISTINCTION EARNED
CONTRIBUTORS

Tyrone Gardiner won the Lightweight Championship of Canada in 1965. He has remained active in boxing circles to this day and has been an inspiration to many the young fighter. After boxing he worked at the county correctional center, operated a gas station, raised horses and occasionally acted as a concert promoter. He enjoys his time now in Mira with his wife Flora, their horses and dog and watching the Eagles hockey games in the winter months.

Charlie Hopkins was a long time friend of the McPhails, and knew Blair Richardson, Ernie Mackinnon and other fighters of the day. He was the first person I interviewed for this book and he verified as well as emphasized how big a deal boxing was in the local area. He worked for many years with the provincial government as Director of Assessment for Cape Breton County. He can often be found around town with his wife Audrey or at his grandkids hockey, soccer or basketball games.

Gordon "Gramps" Kiley was an active fighter in the 1950s and was Maritime Welterweight Champion. After boxing he worked at the Sydney steel plant putting in fifteen years in the blast furnace and twenty years as an electrician. He also was very actively involved in the steelworkers union serving on the executive for many years. He can often be found out walking in Sydney's Ashby District with his wife.

Francis "Rocky" MacDougall won the Featherweight Championship of Canada in 1965. He went on to study at St. Francis Xavier University and worked at first in banking then spent 27 years as an elementary school teacher in Antigonish. He remained quite active in boxing up until 2008 when he was stricken with cancer. He died in 2009.

Eddie McKillop is well known in local circles as a considerable force inside the boxing ring and won numerous championships while a member of the Canadian Armed Forces. He defeated some of Europe's best military boxers during the 1960s. Today he is often seen in the company of Tyrone Gardiner and Rudy Plichie having coffee and discussing the news of the today at their favourite Tim Hortons.

Stan McPhail. spent many of his younger days around boxers, including Gordie MacDougall and Blair Richardson. His father and his brother Walter were also close to the fight scene in Cape Breton. His older brother Dempsey was a boxer and spent many years fighting in the United States. Stan served in the merchant marine during the Second World War and worked for many years at the Sydney Steel Plant. In 2010 his granddaughter and her husband gave him an original restored Model A Ford as a surprise gift.

Rudy Plichie spent numerous years as a cutman and trainer for many local boxers. He was instrumental in keeping the sport alive in Cape Breton and is still often seen at local boxing events. His is a walking encyclopedia on Cape Breton boxing. He spent many years working in the coal mines and was an active member of the mine rescue team.

Hilton Smith fought in the local area before moving to Ontario. He boxed with the Canadian Military winning various accolades and worked with the railway for over thirty years before retiring back to Cape Breton. He became active with the running community and has participated in numerous races, including marathons while well into his seventies. He still can be seen walking or running the streets of Sydney on a daily basis.

Allie Steele fought many boxers on the local scene during the 1950s. After retiring from the ring he became involved in boxing on the administrative side serving with various committees and organizations. Sinclair MacDougall suggested I speak to Allie since he lived only few homes away from me at one time. I never knew he was a boxer. Something I soon learned about many of my other older neighbours. Many of the initial comments Allie made in an interview in 2002 helped form the framework for this book.

Mike Tortola was a longtime resident of New Waterford who could remember the early days of Cape Breton boxing when Joe Uvanni first came to Sydney. Mike ran a very successful dry cleaning business with his brother-in-law Jimmy Giacomantonio in New Waterford for many years. Mike was ninety-three when I had a great conversation with him in 2003. He has since passed on. Photo courtesy of his daughter Lydia Keller.

ACKNOWLEDGEMENTS

Many people have played an important role in helping me bring the story of the great Cape Breton boxers from the ring to the page. Cape Breton University Press editor Mike Hunter's advice, professionalism and attention to detail were a constant source of encouragement. Many thanks are extended to Mike for this support. In the writing and editing department I owe thanks to Allan MacDonald, Ron Caplan, the late Earle Pemberton and numerous sports writers of the past who covered the local fight scene with accuracy, verve and style. The staff of Cape Breton University's archives, the Beaton Institute, provided terrific help with document and photographic research as well as general encouragement over the past several years. They include Catherine Arseneau, Jane Arnold and the two Annes, MacNeil and Connell. The Cape Breton Regional Library deserves credit for supplying years of newspaper microfilm and clippings that proved invaluable. Photographers Blaise Abbass, Ray Doucette and Vaughan Merchant also merit thanks. CBU press editorial and layout staff are worthy of praise for their work. I'd like to thank Dan MacDonald for contributing his wonderful afterword.

From ringside I am indebted to all the boxers, fight fans and boxers' relatives who I interviewed throughout the course of researching this book. Many supplied photographs from their personal collections. I drew on Tyrone Gardiner and Rudy Plichie considerably and wish to thank them for their great memories and ability to recognize fighters in photographs from many decades ago. I'll collectively thank all the other people from whom I sought help, stories and contacts. The long wait for the finished project is finally over. Though some are no longer with us and others aren't as well as when I first met them, together they left me with an overwhelming feeling of athleticism, sportsmanship and camaraderie among a fraternity of gentlemen that I could hardly have imagined existed.

Many people from the local historical circle were very helpful, including Ken Donovan, Peyton Chisholm, Sandra Dunn, Dave MacAulay and especially Bob Morgan for stirring my interest in local history many years ago. Numerous friends as well as colleagues at the University and in the CBU dramagroup have urged me on with this project over the years and I thank them for this. Tony Seed, editor of *Shunpiking* magazine published my first sentence years ago and said to me prior to this, "It's not what you want to write, it's what you want to say." Great advice Tony.

My parents helped me become a reader and my wife and son, Faye and Samuel, allowed me the time to become a writer. I am most grateful to them for this.

P.M.

NOTES

Warmup

1. Mike Tortola, from an interview with the author May 1, 2003.

2. Tony Delvecchio, in "A Split Decision: Italian Boxers of Cape Breton," *Italian Lives, Cape Breton Memories* by Sam Migliore and A. Evo DiPierro, 1999, 252.

3. Clay Moyle, *Sam Langford: Boxing's Greatest Uncrowned Champion.*

4. "Jack Munroe: Pugilist, Prospector, Writer and Soldier of Fortune," by Earle Pemberton. *Punching with Pemberton*, Vol. 2 No. 1, (November) 1961

5. "Mickey MacIntyre: Pride of Cape Breton" by Earle Pemberton. *Punching with Pemberton*, Vol. 1 No. 11, (August) 1961.

6. "A Day with Kid O'Neill" by Earle Pemberton. *Punching with Pemberton*, Vol. 3 No. 7, (September) 1964.

7. "Johnny Gillis: A Review of his boxing career" by Earle Pemberton. *Punching with Pemberton*, Vol. 3 No 9, (Dec-Jan) 1964-1965.

8. "Big Neil J. MacDonald and his seven fighting sons," by Earle Pemberton. *Punching with Pemberton*, Vol. 3 No. 1, (October) 1960.

9. "George Dixon: Only Nova Scotian to win a world championship" by Earle Pemberton. *Punching with Pemberton*, Vol. 3 No. 12.

10. "Joe 'Top Top' Smith: The Guy with the World Boxing Record," by Earle Pemberton. *Punching with Pemberton*, Vol. 1 No. 8 (April) 1961.

11. *Ibid.*

12. George MacEachern, from a transcript of 1978 interview with CBU historian Dr. Donald MacGillvray. MG 19, 21. Beaton Institute, Cape Breton University, Sydney, NS.

13. *The Sydney Post*, May 23, 1923.

14. *George MacEachern: An Autobiography, The Story of a Cape Breton Radical* by George MacEachern, 1987.

15. MacEachern transcript Beaton Institute.

16. From "Johnny Nemis; Ex-Welterweight and Middleweight Champion of the Maritime Provinces" by Earle Pemberton. *Punching with Pemberton*, Vol. 3, No. 6, (August) 1964.

17. "Dominic and James Nemis" in *Italian Lives*, 63-67; and an interview the author had with Sally Durando, November 8, 2009.

18. From an interview with the author November 8, 2009.

19. Kid O'Neill, from "A Day with Kid O'Neill" by Earle Pemberton. *Punching with Pemberton* Vol. 3, No. 7, (September) 1964.

20. Edward Pemberton, from an interview with the author May 26, 2003. Edward was one of Earle Pemberton's four children.

21. From a letter by Fleischer to the editor, *Punching with Pemberton*, Volume 1, Number 10 June-July 1961.

Round One

1. Joe Nemis, from *Italian Lives*, 249-58.

2. From an interview with Sally Durando Nov 8 2009

3 The quote about Johnny Nemis fighting Nedder Healey in New Glasgow is from the *Sydney Post*, Friday, March 12, 1928.

4. From "Johnny Nemis: Ex-Welterweight and Middleweight Champion of the Maritime Provinces" by Earle Pemberton. *Punching with Pemberton*, Vol. 3, No. 6, (August) 1964.

5. Clay Moyle, 392.

6. Allie Steele, from an interview with author, April 11 2003.

7. "Johnny Nemis—Trainer of Champs, in *Cape Breton Post*, October 22, 1964.

8. Sailor Don MacKinnon, *The Fighting Sailor: The Autobiography of Sailor Don MacKinnon, Pride of Saint John, New Brunswick*, 1996.

9. *Ibid.*

10. Benny DeLorenzo, from *Italian Lives*, 254.

11. "Gordie MacDougall, Boxer: My Life" in *Cape Breton Works*, 1996

12. "Johnny Odo—One of Boxing's Best," by Earle Pemberton. *Punching with Pemberton*, Vol. 3 No. 1, 1964.

13. "Johnny Nemis—Trainer of Champs," *Cape Breton Post*, Octobet 22, 1964.

14. From interview with Sally Durando.

15. "Johnny Nemis Dead at 69," by John Campbell. *Cape Breton Post* 1974.

16. From interview with Sally Durando.

17. *Ibid.*

Round Two

1. "George 'Rockabye' Ross, Ex-Canadian Middleweight Champion: A Review of his Career," by Earle Pemberton. *Punching with Pemberton*, Vol. 3, No. 3, 4, 5, 6, 7, 9 and 12 April 1964 to December 1965. This was a special nine-part feature Pemberton wrote on the boxing career of Rockabye Ross.

2. Gordon Kiley, from an interview with the author February 2002.

3. From an article in the *Cape Bretoner Magazine*, September 2002.

4. "A Boxing Memoir: Gramps Kiley" in *Novynka* Vol. 2 No. 1, (January) 2002.

5. Details about Pyle's family and sports and army service background from *Cape Breton Post* obituary Aug 25/09

6. Charlie Hopkins, from an interview with the author January 2002.

7. www.boxrec.com says this fight was a draw.

8. The quotes and comments from Tommy Gun Spencer's daughters are from an article in The *Cape Bretoner Magazine* Sept 2002.

9. Allie Steele interview.

10. Rudy Plichie, from interview with the author.

Round Three

1. The material concerning Ross vs. Durelle and Durelle's post-fight life is from *The Fighting Fisherman: The Life of Yvonne Durelle* (1981). Material on Rockabye Ross from "George 'Rockabye' Ross, Ex-Canadian Middleweight Champion: A Review of his Career," by Earle Pemberton. *Punching with Pemberton*, Vol. 3, No. 12 (December) 1964 – January, 1965.

2. Tyrone Gardiner, from an interview by the author March 2, 2006.

3. Eddie McKillop, from an interview by the author April 27, 2007.

4. Dave LeBlanc, from an interview by the author April 19, 2007.

Round Four

1. "A Boxing Memoir: Gramps Kiley," *Novynka* Vol. 2 No. 1 (January) 2002. Interview by Donalda MacDonald

2. The comments about Mitch Krszwda and Benny Delorenzo are from the unpublished profiles of Cape Breton boxers by Rudy Plichie that he graciously shared with me.

3. Quotes and comments about Gordon Kiley by Rudy Plichie are from his unpublished profiles on Cape Breton boxers.

4. Hilton Smith, from an interview with the author June 14, 2006.

5. Eddie McKillop, from an interview with the author April 27, 2007.

6. Ibid., and from "One Tough Customer: Ed McKillop to be inducted into hall" by Greg MacNeil, *Cape Breton Post* May 26, 2005.

Round Five

1. Joyce Carol Oates, *On Boxing*.

2. Tom Henry, *Inside Fighter*.

3. Tyrone Gardiner, from an interview with the author March 2, 2006.

4. "Tyrone Gardiner: A review of his Boxing Career" by Earle Pemberton in *Punching with Pemberton* Vol. 2 No. 3, 1962.

5. Rudy Plichie, from his unpublished profiles on Cape Breton boxers.

6. McCluskey's comments from *Halifax Champion: Black Power in Gloves, 2005*, 84.

7. Tyrone Gardiner interview.

8. "Tyrone Gardiner" by Earle Pemberton. *Punching with Pemberton*, Vol. 2 No. 3, 1962.

9. Description Gardiner vs. Jones from *Cape Breton Post*, September 9, 1961.

10. Description Gardiner vs. Robert from *Cape Breton Post*, September 30, 1961.

11. Description Gardiner vs. Sprague from *Cape Breton Post*, August 15, 1962.

12. Ibid.

13. Description Gardiner vs. Speight from *Cape Breton Post*, April 19, 1962.

14. Gardiner boxing diary entry about John Cechetto from Peggy MacDonald in the *Highlander*, July 1, 1981.

15. Descriptions of Gardiner vs. Simard from *Cape Breton Post*, and from Aubrey Keizer's "Sportcycle" column, both on November 12, 1962.

16. Tyrone Gardiner, from *Cape Breton Post*, May 18, 1963.

17. Description of Gardiner vs. Sprague from Russ Doyle, *Cape Breton Post*, May 20, 1963.

18. Tyrone Gardiner interview.

19. Rudy Plichie from his unpublished profiles on Cape Breton boxers.

20. Tyrone Gardiner interview; and "Worthy opponents… and a lot of friends," by Peggy MacDonald in the *Highlander*, July 1, 1981.

21. Details about Gardiner vs. Gendron fight are from "Worthy opponents...."

22. Frankie Belanger, *Cape Breton Post*, October 25, 1963.

23. Description of Gardiner vs. Gendron from Russ Doyle, *Cape Breton Post*, October 28, 1963.

24. From "Worthy opponents...."

25. Willie Williams, from a November 18, 2009, phone interview with the author.

26. From Greg MacNeil, *Cape Breton Post*, October 3, 2009.

27. Ibid.

28. Willie Williams interview with the author.

29. From Greg MacNeil, *Cape Breton Post*, October 3, 2009.

30. Willie Williams interview.

31. Details of Gardiner vs. Williams from *Cape Breton Highlander*, June 24, 1964.

32. From Greg MacNeil, *Cape Breton Post*, October 3, 2009.

33. Tyrone Gardiner interview.

34. Gardiner's description of his fight with Ferdinand Chretien is from his (unpublished) presentation to the Old Sydney Society (OSS) in Sydney, NS, March 23, 2006.

35. Description of Gardiner vs. Chretien from *Cape Breton Highlander*, August 5, 1964.

36. The comment about tearing off Chretien's eyebrow and the quote about "wringing the blood…" are from "Worthy opponents…."

37. Tyrone Gardiner, from the OSS lecture (see above).

38. From Greg MacNeil, *Cape Breton Post*, October 3, 2009.

39. "Tyrone Gardiner retains title," by Aubrey Keizer. *Cape Breton Post*, September 7, 1965.

40. From Greg MacNeil, *Cape Breton Post*, October 3, 2009.

41. From Greg MacNeil, *Cape Breton Post*, October 3, 2009.

42. Gardiner's quote about self-confidence is from "Worthy opponents…."

43. From a conversation with the author November 4, 2009.

Round Six

1. "Gordie MacDougall, Boxer: My Life" in *Cape Breton Works*.

2. Leland, from *Halifax Champion*, 15.

3. "Richardson's Boxing Record," by Earle Pemberton. *Punching with Pemberton*, Vol. 2 No. 7, 1962.

4. Nat Fleischer, from "Ring Ramblings" by Wilf McCluskey. *The Unitas Boxing Newsletter*, 1971

5. Stan McPhail, from an interview with the author March 2004.

6. From a conversation with Walter McPhail, August 2009

7. Details about Richardson's 1959 fights and breaking a finger are from "Blair Richardson: A Review of his Boxing Career," by Earle Pemberton. *Punching with Pemberton*, Vol. 2 No.4 (August), 1962.

8. http://boxrec.com/media/index.php?title=Human:26587.

9. From *Halifax Champion*, 15.

10. Description of Buckley's gym from Joe Smith, XXX, April 9, 1980.

11. *Halifax Champion,* 16.

12. From "Blair Richardson: A Review of his Boxing Career."

13. Allie Steele interview.

14. Details about the Al Rose fight and Richardson's broken jaw are from "Blair Richardson: A Review of his Boxing Career."

15. *Halifax Champion,* 16.

16. *Punching with Pemberton,* Vol.1 No. 3, (October) 1960.

17. *Halifax Champion,* 14.

18. Details about Richardson vs. Myrick from *Cape Breton Post* September 28, 1960.

19. Details about Richardson's fights with Cunningham, Turenne, Hamilton and Barnes from "Blair Richardson: A Review of his Boxing Career."

20. Vernon Gilbert, *Cape Breton Post,* May 3, 1961.

21. Charles R. Saunders, *Sweat and Soul,* 1990.

22. *Halifax Champion,* 59.

23. Details about Richardson vs. Emerson from "Blair Richardson: A Review of his Boxing Career."

24. Description of Richardson vs. Emery from Ace Foley, *Cape Breton Post,* August 30, 1961.

25. "Blair Richardson: A Review of his Boxing Career."

26. *Punching with Pemberton,* Vol. 2 No. 1, (November) 1961.

27. Description of Richardson vs. McCoy from "Blair Richardson: A Review of his Boxing Career." The quote about the McCoy fight—"a bone jarring right to the head"—from *Cape Breton Post,* October 31, 1961.

28. Details about Richardson vs. Emery from Ace Foley in the *Halifax Chronicle Herald,* November 28, 1961.

29. "Blair Richardson: A Review of his Boxing Career."

30. "Burned Greaves boxing gloves when he was five" in *Punching with Pemberton,* Vol. 2 No 4, (August) 1962.

31. Aubrey Keizer, "Sportcycle" column, *Cape Breton Post,* June 30, 1962. The comment about needed extra security at the fight is from "Wilf Greaves is 6-5 favorite," *Cape Breton Post,* July 28, 1962.

32. Greaves, from "For the title," *Cape Breton Post,* July 28, 1962.

33. *Halifax Champion,* 17.

34. "Richardson-Greaves" by Earle Pemberton. *Punching with Pemberton* Vol. 2. No. 9, (April-May) 1963.

35. *Halifax Champion,* 18.

36. "Richardson-Greaves."

37. Dave LeBlanc, about witnessing Richardson fight Greaves and then DeNucci, from an interview with the author April 19, 2007.

38. Aubrey Keizer, *Cape Breton Post,* September 30, 1962.

39. Karl Marsh, *Cape Breton Post,* September 30, 1962.

40. "Richardson-Greaves."

41. *Halifax Champion,* 14.

42. *Halifax Champion,* 16.

43. *Halifax Champion,* 17.

44. *Cape Breton Highlander,* June 24, 1964.

45. Ace Foley, *Chronicle Herald,* September XX, 1964.

46. *Halifax Champion,* 17.

47. Ibid.

48. www.cyberboxingzone.com/boxing/Gomeo.htm

49. From "Ring Ramblings" by Wilf McCluskey in *The Unitas Boxing Newsletter,* 1971.

50. From conversations with Gordie Gosse, September 11, 2009, and John MacDonald, September 12, 2009.

51. Rudy Plichie, from an interview with the author April 27, 2007.

52. From "Mourn Passing of Blair Richardson," *Cape Breton Post,* March 5, 1971.

53. From "Richardson-Greaves."

54. The tributes to Richardson after his death from Nemis, MacIsaac and Beaton are form "Pay Tribute to Ring Champ," *Cape Breton Post,* March 7, 1971.

Round Seven

1. Rudy Plichie, from his unpublished profiles of Cape Breton boxers.

2. From an obituary in *Cape Breton Post,* June 13, 2009.

3. Francis "Rocky "MacDougall, from an interview with the author, April 22, 2007.

4. Melvin MacDougall, from an interview with the author October 18, 2009.

5. Aubrey Keizer, *Cape Breton Post*, June 8, 1966.

6. Aubrey Keizer, *Cape Breton Post*, August 4, 1966.

7. From "MacDougall opens camp at Laird gym" by Bob Briscoe. Regina *Leader-Post*, May 27, 1968.

8. John Cechetto as MacDougall's trainer is mentioned in the *Cape Breton Highlander*, April 9, 1966.

9. "Commission want McGrandle examined," *Cape Breton Post*, June 5, 1968; and "McGrandle pulls out, Louis here today" by Bob Briscoe in the Regina *Leader-Post*, June 5, 1968.

10. "McGrandle has eye trouble," Regina *Leader Post*, June 4, 1968.

11. "Unanimous Win, K.O. for MacIntosh" by Aubrey Keizer. *Cape Breton Post*, 1969.

12. "McGrandle aims at third win over MacDougall Thursday" by Ken Jennex. *The Chronicle Herald*, June 29, 1971.

13. "MacDougall retains title" by Ken Jennex. *The Chronicle Herald*, July 2, 1971.

14. Jaime Battiste, from "British Invasion washes up on Cape Breton's shores,"by T. J. Colello. *Cape Breton Post*, May 5, 2007.

15. The quote from Scotty McGrandle is from Billy McGrandle after victory in, *Cape Breton Post*, June 8, 1966.

Round Eight

1. "Gordie MacDougall, Boxer: My Life."

2. Stan McPhail interview.

3. Richard MacKinnon, from a conversation with the author in 2007.

4. Charlie Hopkins interview.

5. From a conversation with the author October 2009

6. From Rudy Plichie's unpublished boxing notes on Cape Breton boxers.

7. Ibid.

Round Nine

1. Rudy Plichie, from "A Split Decision: Italian Boxers of Cape Breton" in *Italian Lives, Cape Breton Memories*.

2. Tyrone Gardiner, from the OSS lecture (see above).

3. Rudy Plichie, from *The Unitas International Boxing News*, date unknown.

4. Plichie's salve to stop a fighter from bleeding and other ringside healing

methods are from his profiles of Cape Breton boxers.

5. Rudy Plichie, from "Les Gillis almost had a shot at world title," *Cape Breton Post*, December 2, 1988.

6. "Cut-man's recipe sweetens metro boxing pot" by Pat Connolly. *Daily News*, December 15, 1991, and "Plichie credited with major role in victory" by Greg Hines. *Cape Breton Post*, January 13, 1992.

7. Tony Unitas, *Unitas International Boxing Newsletter*, 1978.

8. www.ibhof.com/pages/about/inductees/modern/elorde.html.

Round Ten

1. *Cape Breton Post*, June 10, 1967.

2. Kemp MacDonald, from a conversation with the author in 2007.

3. Rudy Plichie are from his unpublished profiles of Cape Breton boxers

4. The quote attributed to Al Bachman about Gussie MacLellan from an interview with Rudy Plichie, April 27, 2007. Other quotes and comments in this chapter from Plichie came from this same interview.

5. Allie Steele interview.

6. Dave LeBlanc interview.

7. "Gussie MacLellan Canada's Premier Boxing Promoter" by Greg Hines. *Cape Breton Post*, November 10, 1979.

8. Ray Doucette, from a conversation with the author September 2009.

9. "Richardson-Graves."

Rematch

1. Brad Ross, from a conversation with the author November 10, 2009.

Future Cards

1. Brad Ross.

Afterword

1. http://sportsillustrated.cnn.com/2006/writers/bill_syken/07/13/scorecard.daily/1.html.

2. http://www.emedicinehealth.com/dementia_in_head_injury/article_em.htm#Dementia%20in%20Head%20Injury%20Overview

3. Varda Burstyn, *The Rite of Man: Manhood, Politics and the Culture of Sport*, 166.

4. Stan Shipley, "Boxing." In *Encyclopedia of World Sport*, 59.

5. Don Morrow and Kevin B. Wamsley, *Sport in Canada: A History*, 22, 32-33.

6. Sugden, 26; Stanley, 61; A.J. Sandy Young, *Beyond Heroes: A Sport History of Nova Scotia*, 26.

7. Sugden, 32; Shipley, 60.

8. Howell, 32. Peter Donnelly, "On Boxing: Notes on the Past, Present and Future of a Sport in Transition," *Current Psychology*, 7. It should also be noted that manliness in this instance was not some subjective aspiration, instead was defined as "a particular middle-class kind of masculinity, and boxing was considered to offer important socialization for youths into manly ideals"; Wamsley and Whitson, 421

9. Gerald Early, *The Culture of Bruising: Essays on Prizefighting, Literature, and Modern American Culture*, 6; Wamsley and Whitson, 21; Sugden, 25.

10. Spears and Swanson, 154; Young, 29.

11. Sammonds, 49-50; See also Jones, 203; Sugden, 33; Wiggins, 185.

12. "Give Us a Fighting Man," *Maritime Labor Herald*, November 1, 1924.

REFERENCES

Books

Ashe, Robert. *Halifax Champion: Black Power in Gloves*. (Halifax, NS: Formac), 2005.

Caplan, Ron, ed. *Cape Breton Works: More Lives from Cape Breton's Magazine*. (Wreck Cove, NS: Breton Books), 1996.

Caprani, Vincent. *Rowdy Rhymes and Rec-im-itations*. (Dublin, Ireland: Mo Publishing), 1982.

Donnelly, Peter. "On Boxing: Notes on the Past, Present and Future of a Sport in Transition."*Current Psychology,* 7 (1988-89).

Early, Gerald. *The Culture of Bruising: Essays on Prizefighting, Literature, and Modern American Culture* (Hopewell, NJ: Ecco Press), 1994).

Fraser, Raymond. *The Fighting Fisherman: The Life of Yvonne Durelle*. (Toronto: Doubleday Canada), 1981.

Henry, Tom. *Inside Fighter: Dave Brown's Remarkable Stories of Canadian Boxing*. (Madeira Park, BC: Harbour Publishing), 2001.

MacEachern, George. *George MacEachern: An Autobiography, The Story of a Cape Breton Radical*. (Sydney, NS: College of Cape Breton Press), 1987.

MacKinnon, Sailor Don and Peter McGahan. *The Fighting Sailor: The Autobiography of Sailor Don MacKinnon, Pride of Saint John, New Brunswick*. (Fredericton, NB: New Ireland Press), 1996.

Maritime Labor Herald, Give Us a Fighting Man," 1 November 1924.

Migliore, Sam and A. Evo DiPiero, eds. *Italian Lives, Cape Breton Memories*. (Sydney, NS: University College of Cape Breton Press), 1999.

Morrow, Don and Kevin B. Wamsley. *Sport in Canada: A History* (Don Mills, ON: Oxford University Press), 2005.

Moyle, Clay. *Sam Langford: Boxing's Greatest Uncrowned Champion*. Seattle, WA: Bennett and Hastings), 2006.

Oates, Joyce Carol. *On Boxing*. Hopewell, NJ: Ecco Press), 1994.

Saunders, Charles R. *Sweat and Soul*. Hantsport, NS: Lancelot Press/Black Cultural Centre for Nova Scotia), 1990.

Shipley, Stan. "Boxing." In *Encyclopedia of World Sport*, edited by David Levinson and Karen Christenson. (New York: Oxford University Press), 1999.

Young, Alexander J. (Sandy). *Beyond Heroes: A Sport History of Nova Scotia*. (Hantsport, NS: Lancelot Press), 1988.

Newspapers, Magazines and Periodicals

Cape Breton Highlander

Cape Breton's Magazine

Cape Bretoner Magazine

Cape Breton Post and its antecedents

Halifax Chronicle Herald

Highlander

Novynka

Punching with Pemberton

Regina Leader-Post

The Chronicle Herald

The Unitas Boxing Newsletter

Internet sources

www.boxrec.com

www.cyberboxingzone.com

A note from the editors;

Sources for many materials reproduced in this book—images, clippings, etc.— could not be positively identified, and therefore due credit is sometimes absent. Cape Breton University Press acknowledges that publications such as the *Cape Breton Post*, the *Chronicle Herald* and *Cape Breton's Magazine* play a vital role in the day-to-day record of people and events in our communities and deserve credit for those efforts. We apologize for those instances where such credit could not, with certainty, be included.

Distinction Earned Index terms

ABOUT THE AUTHOR

Paul MacDougall is a writer of fiction, drama and non-fiction. He has had numerous articles and book reviews published in *Shunpiking*, *The Sunday Herald*, *Cape Bretoner Magazine* and *Pottersfield Portfolio*. In 2008 his memory piece, *The Christmas Catalogue*, was published in the Nimbus anthology, *A Maritime Christmas*. Earlier, his short story *Gambit* (2003) placed second in a fiction contest sponsored by Indigo books and *PEG* was published in the inaugural issue of *Ars Medica* (2004). In 2009 his original one act play *Rockabye* Baby, centred around famed boxer George "Rockabye" Ross, won Best Original Play at the Boardmore Playhouse Festival of One Act Plays held at Cape Breton University. He has four other one act plays, co-written with Ken Chisholm: *O Night Divine* (2005), *All Souls' Eve* (2007) and *Ave Marie* (2008) were each staged at the Boardmore Playhouse Festival of One Act Plays and all won the award for Best Original Play. *Chemical Difference* (2003) won "best play from another source" based on his original short story. Paul is a member of the local CBC radio book panel and is an instructor in health studies at Cape Breton University. He lives in Sydney, NS, with his wife Faye, and their son, Samuel. This is Paul's first book.